The
Belfast & County Down
Railway

Edward M. Patterson

David & Charles
Newton Abbot   London   North Pomfret (Vt)

CONTENTS

1	History	3
2	Motive power and operation	16
3	Road services	30
4	Carriages and wagons	32
5	Two major accidents	38
6	Under the Ulster Transport Authority	40
7	Ulster Transport Authority to Northern Ireland Railways	43
	Bibliography	46
	Appendix: List of stations and halts	46
	Acknowledgements	48

British Library Cataloguing in Publication Data

Patterson, Edward M.
  The Belfast & County Down Railway.
  1. Belfast and County Down Railway.
  2. Railways – Northern Ireland – History
  I. Title
  385′.09416   HE3050.B/

ISBN 0–7153–8306–X

© Edward M. Patterson 1982

All rights reserved. No part of this publication may be reproduced, stored in a retrieval system, or transmitted, in any form or by any means, electronic, mechanical, photocopying, recording or otherwise, without the prior permission of David & Charles (Publishers) Limited

Photoset by
Northern Phototypesetting Co, Bolton
and printed in Great Britain
by Biddles Ltd, Guildford, Surrey
for David & Charles (Publishers) Limited
Brunel House, Newton Abbot, Devon

Published in the United States of America
by David & Charles Inc
North Pomfret, Vermont 05053, USA

Chapter 1

HISTORY

Down is one of the nine counties that formed the ancient province of Ulster. Its area of 957 square miles is bordered to the north and west by Counties Antrim and Armagh, to the south-east it touches County Louth. To the east, a long marine coastline is made by the Irish Sea and by Belfast, Strangford and Carlingford Loughs, while along that seaboard is the most easterly point of Ireland.

Much of Co Down is green farmland, in an undulating landscape of rounded clay hills or drumlins, between which lie level fields, areas of bogland, and little lakes. Higher ground occurs in central and south Down, where granite forms the summits of Slieve Croob and the Mourne Mountains. From Slieve Croob the River Lagan flows towards the north-west among clustered drumlins and then turns north-east along a broad and fertile valley towards its tidal estuary, where the modern city of Belfast is situated.

The coast of east Down lay open to invaders; among the earliest were the Norsemen, who repeatedly raided the area over two centuries following 800 AD. The defenceless old monastery of Bangor was totally destroyed in these attacks. From this troubled period come the Norse names of Strangford and Carlingford. Recovery from this turbulent time was interrupted when the Anglo-Normans made their entry, led by de Courcy. In 1177 he captured the Irish stronghold of Downpatrick, and built a castle near a strategic crossing at the mouth of the River Lagan at a place named Beal Feirste, the ford of the sandbank, now Belfast. English administration strengthened, ruined castles bear mute witness to its grasp, and monasteries were founded at Greyabbey, Blackabbey, Newtownards, Nendrum and Inch. Yet another invasion, this time brief, came from Scotland in 1315, its leader Edward, brother of King Robert I (The Bruce). National Irish influence then strengthened and by the mid-15th century the north of Down was in the hands of the O'Neills of Clannaboye, the English making terms with them. Political expediency made short work of agreements, when Elizabeth I set to overthrow the power of the O'Neill. In retreat, a scorched earth policy was adopted and Sir Brian O'Neill

Above: Belfast, Queen's Quay, the principal station on the B&CD system. The complete reconstruction of the terminus in 1911–12 produced a spacious and well-lit building. A group of soldiers and a pile of kitbags are at the buffers of the new platform 1 and may be setting out for Ballykinlar Camp. (*R. J. Welch*)

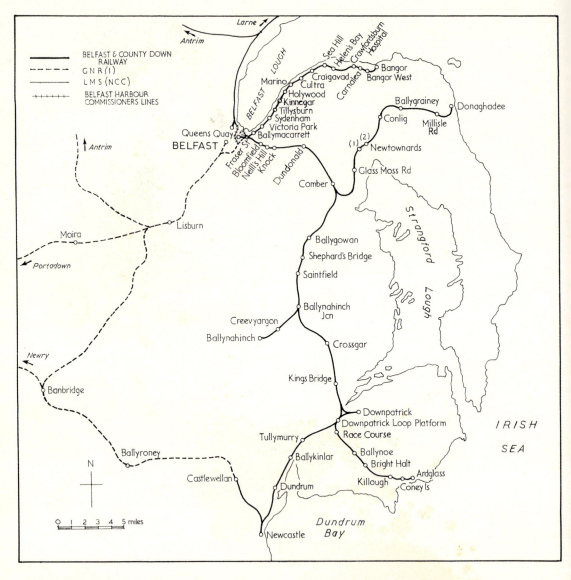

and his men set fire to every remaining monastery and church; 'scarce and starving — a country without happiness and without religion' was the comment of a contemporary traveller in east Down.

Queen Elizabeth took the first steps towards establishing a town at Beal Feirste by making a grant of forfeited lands to Sir Arthur Chichester. In 1613 Belfast received its first Charter of Incorporation from King James I, and had the right to return two members to Parliament. By 1660 it was a thriving market town of five streets. A century later its population was 8,500, by 1810 31,000. Expansion was rapid and by 1900 its homes held 360,000 people; to-day it has topped the half-million. It is Ireland's major industrial city and by far the largest conurbation in Northern Ireland. This swift growth of Belfast was a centripetal process, which resulted in many of the towns in Counties Antrim and Down remaining comparatively small.

On the coast of Down, only Newry in the south had pretensions as a major port; from 1742 it had been linked to Lough Neagh by a canal and soon after that by a short ship canal to Carlingford Lough. Strangford and Portaferry remained mere villages, for though sheltered from the open sea, they were separated by a tide race. In the north-

Above: Ballynahinch Station about 1895. A Vulcan 2–4–0 saddle tank locomotive is about to run round its train. Beyond is a gas cylinder wagon. The bearded figure is guard George Reid. (*Collection of E. M. Patterson*)

east of the county, Donaghadee was the site of a cross-channel packet-station for Scotland, but by 1872 it was eclipsed by Larne. Ardglass, which had housed a trading company in the reign of Henry IV, achieved a reputation as a centre for herring fishing but never grew beyond a population of a thousand.

In the north of Down, Newtownards at the head of Strangford Lough looked out on mud-flats and had no harbour, and Bangor five miles to the north faced the open sea. In the years before the first world war both these places made progress and each had a population of around 10,000; they were exceptions to the general rule. By contrast, 21 miles south-west of Belfast was the county town of Downpatrick: silver coins were minted there in the days of de Courcy, it had its cathedral, court house and gaol, yet Lloyd Praeger, writing a guidebook for the Belfast & County Down Railway in 1904 remarked that 'its appearance now is distinctly dilapidated . . . and factories are falling into decay'.

The County Down railway naturally made its headquarters in the growing city of Belfast. It was the time of the Railway Mania. Its main line went through four small towns en route to Downpatrick and finished on the Mourne shore in 1869 at Newcastle, 38 miles and 10 chains from Belfast.

Thirty-seven years later, an afterthought of a branch went from Newcastle $3\frac{1}{2}$ miles inland, to Castlewellan, meeting the Great Northern Railway there head-on.

Eight miles from Belfast, on the main line, the little town of Comber had a whiskey distillery and a fine market square, and a branch railway ran from there to Newtownards, later to be projected rather circuitously to Donaghadee in quest of the promised Scottish steamer traffic. Government encouragement provided Donaghadee with a splendid harbour, but its twin at Portpatrick in Scotland was far too open to storms to be of any use, and the steamers went to Larne and to Stranraer after a few years.

The most important of the branches went almost from the end of the Belfast platforms to Holywood. Bangor lay eight miles along the coast, but the way was barred by the imperious demands of the Kennedy family, owners of valuable land at Cultra. Bangor might have been reached, most indirectly, by a secondary branch from Conlig, on the line to Donaghadee, but sanity prevailed, and the Holywood–Bangor link was forged, though forcibly warped inland and up steep gradients, from Kennedy's saleable shore.

Midway between Comber and Downpatrick a short branch ran from nowhere in particular four miles to the small market town of Ballynahinch. There were spa wells nearby, but neither a Harrogate nor a Cheltenham arose in spite of fond hopes.

Above: Before reconstruction in 1911–12 Queen's Quay terminus seems to have been a gloomy station beneath a low-slung roof of heavy timbering. The County Down never ran refreshment cars but suggestions to slake the thirsts of arriving passengers loomed overhead as he and his family ran for a cab. *(R. J. Welch)*

Right: Bloomfield station was opened in 1879 and was only 1½ miles from Queen's Quay. The cost of the station was contributed by property owners in the area. The view looks towards Knock. (*Courtesy National Library of Ireland*)

Below: Seen on a wintry day in 1894 Queen's Quay terminus possessed a distinguished appearance. The reconstruction work of 1911–12 added wings to left and right of the façade, and effectively doubled its size. What appears to be the old BH&BR terminus is glimpsed to the left. *(R. J. Welch – Ulster Museum)*

Much later than the others, Castlewellan excepted, a seven mile branch joined Downpatrick with Ardglass, running through unpromising and rather bleak farmland. Hopefully in search of herring, a short extension crept down to the harbour, but was little used and was lifted before many years had passed.

Born during the Railway Mania of the 1840s, the Belfast & County Down Railway was bound to have competitors within the county. Almost simultaneously, there arose the Great County Down Railway, the Newry, Warrenpoint & Rostrevor Railway, the Newry, Banbridge & Belfast Junction Railway, and the Holywood Atmospheric Railway. The first of these, fully titled the Great County Down, Belfast, Newry and Warrenpoint Railway, was provisionally registered in the summer of 1845. It was promoted by a splendid array of noblemen, landowners,

clergy and not least by merchants, mostly from Newry, but none from Belfast. Its line was to run from Warrenpoint, through Newry and Banbridge, with a westerly artery heading to join the Ulster Railway at Moira, and another sweeping through Rathfryland, Castlewellan, Downpatrick and Comber, en route to Belfast. It never got beyond the preliminaries.

On 25 February 1845 in the Donegall Arms Hotel, Belfast there was held 'a meeting of parties favourable to the promotion of a railway to Holywood, Comber and Newtownards'. Such was the first infant cry of what was to be the Belfast & County Down Railway. A month later the promoters decided to obtain powers to extend to Downpatrick. There began weary months of argument between the B&CD backers and those who were behind the Great County Down project. The B&CD committee were astute businessmen and were wary of entanglements. The Atmospheric promoters were bought off, and gave up their application for an Act. Some measure of compromise was reached between the GCD and the B&CD and when the former placed its Bill before Parliament it failed to comply with Standing Orders and was withdrawn. The NWRR obtained its Act, but it was free of the B&CD's field of action. The NB&BJR scheme died at birth, but much later arose, phoenix-like, as a fragment of the Great Northern. The Belfast & County Down promoters emerged as victors in the east of the county, and their Act obtained the Royal Assent on 26 June 1846. For the provisional committee the way was clear to raise funds for construction. The authorised capital was £500,000.

The plans for the railway authorised by the 1846 Act, show a section of main line that was never built. Beyond Comber it was to have been made just west of the main Killinchy–Killyleagh road and it would have had eleven level crossings. Nearing Downpatrick it was to have crossed the tidal estuary of the River Quoile 'by means of a Bridge supported on Wooden or Iron Piles, and not on Piers' because of possible interference with a tide mill belonging to a Mr Maxwell.

The gathering of capital was slow, and the directors wisely decided to restrict construction to the Belfast–Newtownards and the Belfast–Holywood portions, and not to attempt to reach Donaghadee or Downpatrick. Contracts were let to William Dargan. The level, lough-side, line to Holywood was the first to be finished and was opened to traffic on 2 August 1848. The *Belfast News Letter* reported:

> HOLYWOOD RAILWAY – This branch of the Belfast and County Down Railway was first opened to public traffic on Wednesday. The line runs parallel with the Belfast Bay, on the County Down side, and being a perfect level, the movement is very easy. The carriages are fitted up very elegantly and with every regard for comfort. The arrangements for the transfer of traffic are carried out with the utmost satisfaction and punctuality.

Meanwhile William Dargan's men had excavated deep cuttings through the gravelly soil in the gap between the Holywood and Castlereagh Hills, and thence to Comber. The line rose at a gradient of 1 in 197 for $1\frac{1}{2}$ miles to a summit near the village of Knock, $3\frac{1}{2}$ miles from the terminus. Dundonald, five miles out, was on a falling gradient and Comber was three miles beyond it, and a mile from the salt water of Strangford Lough. Construction then forsook the main line, the Newtownards branch curved sharply towards the north, running level for three miles before climbing at 1 in 100 to a temporary terminus near Scrabo Hill west of the town. Trains ran there from 6 May 1850.

Steady traffic began to build up and the Board rewarded the shareholders with a modest dividend of 2% while their position was consolidated. To take the main line beyond Comber it was now necessary to seek a renewal of the Parliamentary powers, for these had lapsed. The necessary Act was obtained on 28 May 1855, it also formally reconstituted the Company, and reduced the number of directors from 13 to eight. Reference has already been made to the realignment which the new Act permitted, a wise decision since the three small towns on the new route (Ballygowan, Saintfield and Crossgar) offered more traffic potential than had the original scheme. However, the 1855 line needed considerable effort in construction as there were numerous deep rock cuttings and the company was now required to take enough land to accommodate a double line of rails, and overbridges were double width. The tender for the extension went to a contractor named Moore. Part of the line was opened for traffic on 10 September 1858 to the branch terminus at Ballynahinch. From the junction, $3\frac{1}{2}$ miles from Ballynahinch, work went on and the line was opened through to the county town on 23 March 1859. All of it was single track.

In both the 1846 and 1855 schemes, Bangor was to have been reached by a branch leaving the Donaghadee line near Conlig, entering Bangor from the south and with a terminus at the quay. But the directors were shrewd enough to see that Bangor had growth potential and were unhappy about reaching it over 20 miles rather than 12. Some years were allowed to slip by until, by an Act of 12 June 1861, the entire Bangor branch was abandoned. History had overtaken it and a rival, if friendly company was on the scene, the Belfast, Holywood & Bangor Railway. This concern had persuaded landowners and Parliament to let them build from Holywood to Bangor, logically and directly along the south side of, if not the shore of Belfast Lough. Three years were allowed for completion of the eight miles of railway, and the authorised capital was to be £115,000, with borrowing powers of £38,000. At Holywood the

Dundonald station. No 26 brings in the 12.50 pm down Comber train on a summer day in the 1930s (*W. Robb*)

BHBR line was to join the existing County Down line a short distance west of the latter's station. To satisfy the landowners, there were two noteworthy stations. Cultra was to be 'of an ornamental character' and 'at least One Half of the Trains' were to stop there, failing which the company was to be liable to a penalty of ten pounds a day. A further amenity for the local clientele was a covered footbridge across the tracks, the sole example on the entire system. Helen's Bay station was the remarkable result of the influence of Baron Dufferin and Clandeboye on the environment of his estate. The main station building was built on the single line (now the 'down' platform after doubling) in Scottish baronial style, complete with crow-stepped gables and a cloistered façade. There was a private waiting room for Lord Dufferin, and from it a long flight of stone steps, originally roofed, led down to a hexagonal courtyard through which passed an avenue that linked Clandeboye House to the shore. The avenue, tree-lined along its four-mile length, passed under the railway by a splendid ornamental archway, faced with massive heraldic crests and bearing a pair of projecting stone turrets. A third, more massive turret rose at the head of the covered stairway and was capped by a slated spire. Public approach to the station lay across a broad square, which for many years accommodated the village shoemaker's premises in a wooden hut.

A mile beyond the glories of Helen's Bay station, the line crossed Crawfordsburn Glen on a five-arched sandstone viaduct. A brief glimpse of tree tops through the trellised iron parapets brought the passengers through a twin-arched bridge on a short up-grade, and across open fields to Carnalea. The original station here was merely a disused wagon body, adequate for the sparse traffic in an area still largely open country. Two cuttings brought the line to its Bangor terminus at Catherine Place, opposite the estate wall of Bangor Castle. The BHBR needed to get Parliamentary

From the BH&BR in 1884 the County Down inherited a single platform terminus at Bangor. Six years later it was rebuilt and gave the town their first taste of Italianate brickwork, and the luxury of three platforms, though the fine tower never acquired clock faces. Sadly the UTA failed to appreciate this interesting building and speedily reduced it to a cubist nonentity. (*Courtesy National Library of Ireland*)

authority for an extension of time in July 1863, the Act giving the company additional powers to build a hotel and refreshment rooms at Bangor station, public baths and a marine promenade. The extension to Bangor carried traffic from mid-May 1865.

From 1859 the County Down company's finances were in an increasingly unhappy state. No dividends had been paid on either the Ordinary or the Preference shares, and in an attempt to lift itself out of its monetary slough the company sold its Holywood branch to the BHBR company for £50,000, thus giving the Bangor company access to the city. In addition the County Down received an annual rent of £5,000 from the Bangor company, which had to build itself a separate station at Queen's Quay with its own access and booking office, the BCDR paying £400 of the cost. In the agreement the Bangor company was not permitted to extend its railway to Donaghadee nor to compete with the Co Down's traffic to that town.

From Newtownards, where the County Down had rested since May 1850, there was increasing urgency to see the completion of the branch to Donaghadee, for that place was finding favour as a cross-channel port. The contract was let to Edwards. Newtownards' first station was by-passed, the line rising on an embankment on which it swept around the north of the town. A gradient of 1 in 100 took it out of Newtownards, curving north to a gable just south of the village of Conlig. A short-lived station was built there to serve the dower house of the Dufferin family. Near the road junction of Six Road Ends, a station was built, at first named Groomsport & Bangor, then Groomsport Road, and finally Ballygrainey. From there the last few miles to the coast ran over peat-

The front of Donaghadee station in 1935. (*David L. Smith*)

moss and through some short rock cuttings, then curved sharply towards the north to the terminus, sited on the sea-front at the back of a singularly banal terrace house. Construction of the magnificent harbour was still in progress, when the railway opened on 3 June 1861. The harbour works were a massive blend of grey Anglesey limestone, and brown Mourne granite, and were completed in 1863 at a cost to the Treasury of £150,000.

The distance from Donaghadee to the Scottish coast at Portpatrick was 20 miles, and spasmodic public sailings had been made across that stretch of sea for over a century. There was a growing need for a regular timetable service and since the introduction of the Universal Penny Post in 1839, the Post Office required dependable conveyance for a growing volume of mail. In spite of primitive harbour facilities a mail steam packet service had operated between Portpatrick and Donaghadee from 1825 until 1849. Reliability of the service improved as steamers became more powerful, and during the 1830s there were over 10,000 passengers a year on the route, many being itinerant labourers. But an increasing body of criticism was being levelled against Portpatrick harbour, as being cramped, exposed and unsafe, sited on the rocky west-facing coast of the Rhinns of Galloway. Cairnryan was being suggested as a safer alternative, while the Stair family of Castle Kennedy attempted to push Stranraer. By the time the Donaghadee branch was opened, there was increasing uncertainty whether a regular steamer service would ever develop between there and Portpatrick. A twice-weekly steamer was sailing between Stranraer and Belfast. Direct opposition to Donaghadee as a port was coming from the Belfast & Northern Counties Railway which was linked with the Carrickfergus & Larne Railway. That company's line was opened to passengers on 1 October 1872 to Larne Harbour, but for four years the town-to-harbour line was little used. Meanwhile the harbour at Portpatrick was being repeatedly battered by storms. In 1873 the Board of Trade cast off its responsibility for maintaining it, and passed it to the local authority. With neither money nor incentive to maintain the harbour works deterioration continued. In the end Donaghadee Harbour remained in a splendid state of sheltered disuse, unable to divert the established mail boats from the Stranraer–Larne run, and unable to offer the County Down Railway any traffic from 'across the water'. The double overbridges continued to span the single track.

As early as 1861 an extension beyond Downpatrick seemed a possibility, when a concern named the Downpatrick & Newry Railway Company obtained Royal Assent to a link between the County Down line and the little Newry, Warrenpoint & Rostrevor Railway, both of which were to provide capital. The scheme did not mature and another five years were to pass before the Downpatrick, Dundrum & Newcastle Railway Act provided an attenuated alternative. The DD&NR was to strike towards the coast of Dundrum Bay, pass the shadow of the ivy-clad ruins of one of de Courcy's great Norman castles at Dundrum itself and continue thence across seaside links into Newcastle, a small town set against the Mourne Mountains, scenically in a superb situation and with considerable tourist potential. A contemporary guide book mentioned a spa well, and referred to Newcastle as 'the Scarborough of Ireland' though, fortunately perhaps, it never acquired that place's barrage of boarding houses.

The Downpatrick, Dundrum & Newcastle's Act was dated 10 August 1866, and capital was to be £75,000, with the usual borrowing powers. A later Act of 25 June 1868 reduced the capital to £60,000, and allowed the County Down company to contribute £10,000 and to work the proposed line. O'Connor & Olley were the contractors, and the line was opened in March 1869. After working the line for 12 years, the County Down bought it for £12,000 in cash, plus the issue to the Newcastle company of £38,000 in debenture shares.

Once the railway was opened to Newcastle the town flourished in a modest way as a seasonal tourist centre. The railway company assisted the process, encouraging the formation of a golf club, the course ranging along the links between the railway and the shore, by paying £382 for the erection of a golf club house, and by building pavilions near the station goods sidings for the use of excursion parties. The zenith of tourist expansion came in 1898 when the County Down Railway opened its imposing Slieve Donard Hotel, with five floors and 120 bedrooms set by the shore in spacious shrubby grounds at the northern edge of the town. Its glowing red brick made it a landmark, but many thought that the warm brown granite of Mourne would have been a more appropriate building material.

The burgeoning of Newcastle caused the Great Northern Railway to cast envious eyes on tourist movements, and the County Down Railway to look a little apprehensively over its shoulder. The Great Northern was a far more powerful company than the County Down, and it already had a branch line through the town of Banbridge, 18 miles north-west of Newcastle, which ended at a hamlet named Ballyroney only 10 miles from Newcastle. Not surprisingly the Great Northern sought powers to lay its line beyond Ballyroney through Castlewellan and down to the coast at Newcastle. The County Down argued, none too convincingly against the GN's proposals in parliament, while the GN stood poised to advance into territory which the County Down had thought to be its own. In the end a compromise was reached: the Great Northern was to extend from Ballyroney to Castlewellan, and the County Down to construct a spur from Newcastle to Castlewellan. The County Down had asked for running powers over the Great Northern as far as Scarva but had to be satisfied with running powers from Castlewellan to Ballyroney, which were of no practical use to it and which were never utilised. Messrs Fisher & le Fanu was the contractor for the Castlewellan branch of the County Down. With the entry of Great Northern trains into Newcastle

Newcastle station was completely rebuilt in 1906. Passengers found themselves confronted with an incongruous red brick building that was presided over by a massive clock-tower that seemed to belong to a church or a castle rather than a railway. The front of the building was defaced by an enormous glazed portico that might have been appropriate to a city terminus but did little to shelter the squadron of jaunting cars awaiting the arrival of a train and its tourists. (*Courtesy National Library of Ireland*)

from 24 March 1906 that terminus became invested with the subtly distinctive air of a joint station, though in fact it was a purely County Down station, and the Great Northern was there only by virtue of the running powers which Parliament had given it over the County Down's branch. On the other hand, Castlewellan really was a joint station, where the two lines met end-on, the County Down maintaining the loop and the Great Northern the station buildings and signals. Castlewellan station staff were joint employees and their uniforms, appropriately faced were supplied year-about by the two companies.

Back along the shore of Belfast Lough, the history of the Holywood to Bangor extension line was to be anything but simple. As we have seen, the Belfast, Holywood & Bangor company bought the County Down's branch line to Holywood in 1865, and operated trains from the city into Bangor, the final eight miles being single line. Eight years of that and the Bangor company found itself heavily in debt and under-capitalised, and realising that further independent operation would be profitless it effected a lease of its line to the County Down in August 1873. Arrangements were made to pay off the Bangor company's debts, notably those to the Midland Wagon Company which was involved in complicated leasing arrangements over rolling stock. In return the BHBR was to receive an annual payment of £4,000 increasing to £5,000 in 1878. The sickly existence of the Bangor company continued for a few more years until by an Act of 14 July 1884 the Bangor company's assets were transferred to the County Down. The six engines with which the BHBR had worked its line were taken into BCDR stock and renumbered. The two adjacent stations at Queen's Quay were merged in November 1884 by the simple expedient of breaking an archway through the dividing wall. For 12 years the County Down worked the Holywood–Bangor section as a single line with a passing loop at Craigavad. As traffic increased, the single line became an embarassment, and the section was doubled in stages between 1897 and 1902.

The branch to Ardglass came into being as a result of indirect Government aid to the herring fishing industry and an Order in Council was approved on 29 November 1890 under the Light Railways (Ireland) Act 1889. Ardglass was already a busy fishing port with most of its modest population of 550 connected with the herring industry. Its roots went back to the Norman invasion when it was an important landing place, and at that time de Courcy built no fewer than seven castles around the harbour. Nearby was the village of Killough, with a tiny harbour, a few fishing boats and a brickworks. The Ardglass branch left the main line just south of Downpatrick, progressing through typically hummocky farmland over which the line was laid as inexpensively as possible, with the minimum of earthworks, and numerous short, steep gradients. There were no fewer than five level crossings in its course of seven miles. A station was placed two miles from Downpatrick at Ballynoe; there was no village there and its claim to fame was a well-preserved prehistoric stone circle nearby. Beyond the terminus at Ardglass a steeply graded extension wound down to the harbour, so that fishing boats might unload directly into wagons. It was little used and was abandoned after some years.

Apart from Newcastle, the County Down was aware of a Great Northern presence half a mile from its Belfast terminus where what was referred to as 'The Central' ran in close to Ballymacarrett Junction. The Belfast Central Railway got its Act on 25 July 1864, with the laudable intention of joining the Ulster, the Belfast & Northern Counties and the County Down companies to a centrally situated station, not an easy matter in a rapidly expanding city where land was expensive. The Central was soon in financial trouble. New directors and a new Act forced the work forward in 1872, but with reduced objectives. In its final form, the BCR started from a junction half a mile from the Great Northern (formerly the Ulster) terminus, and ran to a cottage-like terminus of its own at the western end of Queen's Bridge. Half a mile before Queen's Bridge, a branch crossed the River Lagan into County Down territory. Central trains could only enter the neighbouring companies' termini by reversal. Three years before the Central opened, street tramways began to operate in the city and sealed the fate of the Central. In August 1885 the Central sold out to the Great Northern, which promptly ended passenger working in November. A short tunnel under the end of Queen's Bridge eventually linked the Central to the Northern Counties, over Harbour Commissioners' lines, making it a useful goods appendage to the three main line companies, for wagon transfer. Passenger specials were occasionally worked from the Great Northern on to the County Down lines, until the line was cut in

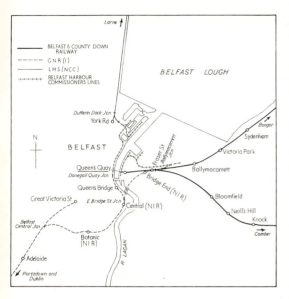

1965 to allow road improvements. A governmental change of heart brought a reconnection in 1976 under the nationalised ownership of Northern Ireland Railways, a revitalisation that forms a postscript to this main story.

Between 1848 and the present day, the County Down line in its broadest sense had 51 stations. Four (Tullymurry, Newtownards, Conlig and Glenmachan) had been closed after comparatively short periods of use. Only Ballynahinch Junction and Downpatrick Loop had island platforms, the latter recalling Cairnie Junction on the Great North of Scotland Railway in having no road access. Remarkably, no fewer than ten stations had subways linking the platforms; they were at Neill's Hill, Dundonald, Comber, Saintfield, Crossgar, Castlewellan, Newtownards, Holywood, Helen's Bay and Carnalea. Level crossings were unusually few in number, except as noted on the Ardglass branch.

Participation and part-ownership in coastal steamers had been firmly frustrated by the collapse of the Donaghadee–Portpatrick project. Nevertheless the County Down company provided a paddle steamer service on Belfast Lough, mainly between the city and Bangor, from June 1893. It probably based this enterprise on a clause in the Belfast, Holywood & Bangor Act of 1881, which permitted that company to operate steam vessels 'for the purpose of establishing an improved and efficient communication between Belfast, Holywood and Bangor'. The BH&BR never ran lough steamers but the desire to do so sprang from a long and varied background. The original 'Bangor Boat' was a tiny paddler named *Greenock* which on 19 April 1816 became the first steamer to cross between Scotland and Ireland. She was in the lough for about a month. Dr D. B. McNeill has chronicled the history of 24 privately run vessels which operated local services from the *Greenock*'s advent until the early 1890s. The County Down Railway took advice from the experienced Glasgow & South Western Railway which was having a paddle steamer *Glen Rosa* built at Clydebank by Messrs J. & G. Thompson. The BCDR ordered its twin from Thompson's, named her *Slieve Donard* after the highest of the Mourne Mountains, and put her into service on 20 June 1893. With Captain Dalzell Torrance as master, she sailed from Donegall Quay in the city, a long stone's throw from Queen's Quay terminus, down the lough to Bangor, with occasional trips to Larne and Donaghadee.

The response of the public to the railway steamer was so encouraging that an order for a second paddler was placed with Thomson's yard in October 1893, and this steamer made her trial trip on 1 May 1894, under the name *Slieve Bernagh*, which is the second highest summit of the Mourne Mountains. Capt Torrance assumed command, while Capt McCorquodale took over *Slieve Donard*. For five years the two steamers were operated until in 1899 the company sold *Slieve Donard* out of the lough to Messrs P. & A. Campbell for £12,500, when she worked as *Albion* in the Bristol Channel and on the south coast of England. She was commandeered as a minesweeper, HMS *Albyn* in 1915, survived the war and was broken up in 1921.

Slieve Bernagh continued to serve on the lough sailings on her own for 12 years, with occasional trips on excursions to Portaferry, Ardglass, Larne and Portrush. Then at the end of the 1911 season she was offered for sale through a firm of Glasgow shipbrokers for £12,000. A ready sale did not materialise and by the end of the year the board minutes mention a price of £10,000, then it slid to £7,000 and finally she was sold to Messrs D. & J. Nicol of Dundee on 19 June 1912 for what must have been the disappointing sum of £4,350. Nicols used her without change of name on the Forth sailings on the east coast of Scotland until the outbreak of the first world war when she returned to Dundee. The Admiralty requisitioned her in October 1917, for a time she became Hospital

Carrier *HC5*, and was broken up at Inverkeithing during 1923.

Slieve Bernagh was replaced by the last of the County Down's ships, the paddle-steamer *Erin's Isle*, built for the company by Messrs A. & J. Inglis of Glasgow at a cost of £24,000. Launched on 12 June 1912, a hectic month of fitting out followed before she went into service on the lough on 12 July, the *Bernagh* having been given a quick overhaul at the Queen's Island to maintain services in the earlier part of that summer. After four seasons on the lough the *Erin's Isle* tied up at Dufferin Dock on 29 September 1915. Nine days later she was inspected by the Admiralty and on 20 November requisitioned at £400 per month. Six days later she sailed from Belfast under naval orders.

Erin's Isle served her country as a minesweeper but was never to return to her owners. A letter from the Admiralty on 19 February 1919 told that she had been mined and sunk. The company considered a replacement but found that it would cost £64,000. In May 1919 the Admiralty admitted liability for £53,676. With this capital compensation, and the monthly rental, the owners must have had few regrets over their purchase seven years before. With her going the company's interest in steamboat operation was over. By the 1920s the popularity of local sailings, restricted by a short season, was fading.

All the County Down Railway's steamers had twin compound diagonal engines and their relevant dimensions were:

DOWN TRAINS.—WEEK DAYS.

Distances from Belfast Miles.		1	2	3	4	5	6	7	8
		Goods	Pass.	Pass.	Light Engine	Pass.	Pass.	Pass.	Goods
		A.M.	A.M.	A.M.	NOON.	P.M.	P.M.	P.M.	P.M.
	BELFAST,	6 0	8 0	10 35	—	1 45	4 50	7 35	10 0
2¾	Knock,	—	8 7	10 42	—	*F*	4 57	7 42	—
5	Dundonald,	—	8 15	10 49	—	1 58	5 5	7 49	—
8	Comber, arr.	6 25	8 24	10 58	—	2 5	5 14	7 58	10 30
	Comber, dep. for	6 30	8 30	11 5	12 0	2 10	5 19	8 3	—
12	Scrabo, Siding	6 50	—	—	12 15	—	—	—	—
13½	Newtownards,	6 55	8 43	11 20	—	2 25	5 32	8 18	—
15¾	Conlig,	—	*	—	—	—	5 38	—	—
17¾	Groomsport,	—	8 58	—	—	—	5 47	8 30	—
22	Donaghadee,	—	9 8	—	—	—	6 0	8 43	—
	Comber, dep. for	—	8 27	—	—	2 7	5 16	8 0	10 45
12	Ballygowan,	—	8 39	—	—	2 19	5 28	8 12	11 15
15¼	Saintfield,	—	8 47	—	—	2 27	5 36	8 20	11 35
17¾	Ballynahinch Jc.	—	8 54	—	—	2 37	5 44	8 28	11 50
21¼	Crossgar,	—	9 5	—	—	2 48	5 55	8 37	12 20
26¾	Downpatrick,	—	9 23	—	—	3 5	6 15	8 55	12 45

Donaghadee Goods to be sent by No. 7 Train. *F* Stops on Fridays only.
No. 1 takes Passengers to Newtownards on Saturdays.
Ballynahinch Waggons containing Goods to be sent by No. 7 Train.

DOWN TRAINS.—SUNDAYS.

Distance from Belfast. Miles.	STATIONS.	1	2	3	
		Passengers.	Passengers.	Passengers.	
		A.M.	P.M.	P.M.	
	BELFAST, . . .	9 25	2 15	7 35	—
2¾	Knock, . . .	9 32	2 22	7 42	—
5	Dundonald, . . .	9 40	2 30	7 49	—
8	Comber, . . . arr.	9 49	2 38	7 58	—
	Comber, . . . dep.	9 55	2 40	8 3	—
13½	Newtownards, . .	10 10	2 55	8 18	—
15¾	Conlig, ...	—	—	—	—
17¾	Groomsport and Bangor, .	10 23	—	8 30	—
22	Donaghadee, . . .	10 35	—	8 43	—
	Comber, . . . dep.	9 52	—	8 0	—
12	Ballygowan, . . .	10 4	—	8 12	—
15¼	Saintfield, . . .	10 12	—	8 20	—
17¾	Ballynahinch Junction, .	10 20	—	8 28	—
21¼	Crossgar, ...	10 32	—	8 37	—
26¾	Downpatrick, . . .	10 50	—	8 55	—

	Gross Tons	Length – ft	Beam – ft	Draught – ft	Speed – knots
Slieve Donard	360	200	25	9	17
Slieve Bernagh	383	225	26	9	17
Erin's Isle	630	225	29	9	17

The most intensive steamer services operated when the *Slieve Donard* and *Slieve Bernagh* were both at work. On weekdays, including Saturdays, there were six sailings from Belfast to Bangor, a 55min journey. The first sailing was at 10.30, the last at 18.30. Going up the lough, the first boat from Bangor left at 8.00, the last at 19.45. A mid-afternoon boat continued from Bangor to Donaghadee where it spent 15 minutes before returning. Saturday afternoon sailings from Belfast to Bangor went across the lough to Larne, giving a one hour call there and a total journey time for city folk of almost six hours. On Sundays there were five departures from Belfast.

The company's participation in the extending tourist trade mainly involved Newcastle. The little town had grown steadily since the first railway came there in 1869, and the Mourne Mountains provided not only a dramatic backdrop, but gave the more energetic the challenge of hard walking and an ascent of Slieve Donard. By the 1890s the company was at the peak of its financial strength, as evidenced by its ventures into steamships. It was decided to open a railway hotel at Newcastle,

Left: A part of the BCDR working timetable dated 3 November 1862. The calls at the Scrabo Stone siding, and at the short-lived station of Conlig, are noteworthy. Downpatrick was the southern terminus.

Above: A view from the temporary bridge at Glass Moss Road level crossing during the 1932 Tourist Trophy Race. The Glass Moss–Donaghadee train is at the platform on the north side of the crossing with locomotive No 12 at the near end and No 26 at the far end. The driver of No 12 views the race from his cab roof. Car No 34 (E. R. Hall MG) is approaching at high speed. (*Courtesy of the 'Autocar'*)

and already the first steps had been taken in the 1881 Act of Parliament which transferred the DD&N Railway to the BCDR. Further powers were obtained in 1891 covering hotels at Bangor, Ardglass and Ballynahinch, none of which was built. But the Newcastle hotel, christened *The Slieve Donard* with five floors and 120 bedrooms was the most imposing structure of its kind in Ireland. It was opened with an appropriate amount of pomp and circumstance by the Countess of Annesley on 21 June 1898. Capital expenditure on the hotel between 1894 and 1899 totalled £94,000. A few years earlier the railway company had helped the infant golf club at Newcastle by spending £382 on the erection of a club house, which it rented to the club. It backed these with the introduction of the Saturday midday train, named The Golfers' Express, running non-stop to Newcastle, and giving businessmen and their families an appetising rattle through the countryside of Down before luncheon.

A great tourist attraction, which involved the BCDR closely for nine years, was the Royal Automobile Club's Tourist Trophy Race. Initiated in the Isle of Man in 1905, it was revived after a lapse of many years in 1928 on a $13\frac{1}{2}$ mile triangular road circuit that linked the towns of Dundonald, Newtownards and Comber. The County Down main line crossed the race circuit no less than four times: on bridges at Dundonald station, Comber station and at the site of the earlier Newtownards station, and at Glass Moss level-crossing $1\frac{1}{2}$ miles from Comber towards Newtownards. Enormous crowds travelled to watch both at morning practice sessions in midweek, and on 'race Saturday'. Cheap excursion fares were offered to the three towns on the course, and the railway built a semi-permanent grandstand at Comber, charging 10s (50p) for a seat, tea and a public broadcast. The charge was later reduced to 7s 6d (32p) for the seat alone.

The Glass Moss crossing prevented the working of through trains between Comber and Newtownards. The problem was handled by cancelling the Tyers Tablet working during the time the public roads were closed. Two trains took over the working of the branch, one shuttling between Comber and the south side of Glass Moss crossing, the other between the north side of the crossing and Donaghadee, $12\frac{3}{4}$ miles distant. Both trains had an engine at each end, and a pilotman was on the leading engine in each case. Passengers transferred from one train to the other via a substantial wooden overbridge, erected at Glass

Moss for race week. A short way on each side of the gates two temporary wooden platforms were built, though as these were only the length of three carriages and trains were usually made up to eleven, the trains had to be brought up in stages to allow passengers to alight. The lower quadrant signals protecting the crossing were left in the danger position during the race, and were passed for a short distance on the authority of the pilotman. On the longer run from Glass Moss to Donaghadee, the train was worked by two engines only as far as Newtownards. Arriving there the banking engine, a 4-4-2T, went to the head of the train, while the leading engine (an 0-6-0, usually No 26) uncoupled and remained at Newtownards to assist the train in rear to Glass Moss on its return. The tank engine could thus take water at Donaghadee, while the tender engine did less work and could last until late afternoon, when it went to Donaghadee for water before returning to Belfast. Four down trains were affected by this working.

Though Glass Moss was not a recognised stop at any other time, passengers were able to book to it during the race event. A temporary ticket office was set up, and once there passengers took full advantage of the excellent roadside view. Any who dallied on the bridge, which made a most spectacular viewpoint, were quickly moved on by police and railwaymen.

The TT seemed set to be a perpetual event, but in 1936 a serious crash occurred in Newtownards, killing nine spectators who were thronging the footpath. As a result the circuit was deemed unsafe, and no further events took place on it. There can have been no other car racing circuit in the world, where a railway was so intimately and so profitably involved.

Of the County Down's general managers, the most illustrious was Joseph Tatlow, who spent five years at Queen's Quay from the late 1880s and by his efforts hauled the company back to an organised prosperity after years of mediocre management. But the best remembered was undoubtedly William Frederick Minnis JP who joined the company in July 1884 as a boy of 12 to start as an apprentice clerk in the general manager's office. He subsequently served as booking clerk, parcels clerk, assistant in the traffic superintendent's office and relief station agent. From the variety of that last job, he was made clerk in charge of the Belfast booking office, and then in 1897 goods agent at Belfast. Seven years later, when C. A. Moore became general manager, Minnis moved up to fill the position of traffic superintendent. He was made general manager in 1926, and saw the company through much of the second world war, retiring in July 1944 after 60 years of service. Billy Minnis had two ways of relaxing — golf and gardening; he favoured the nine-hole course at Helen's Bay for the first of these, but a visit to his home at Knock was to sense his enthusiasm for roses and carnations. Throughout the year, he was well known for the flower in his buttonhole.

Chapter 2

MOTIVE POWER AND OPERATION

It is unfortunate that before the second world war no accurate and complete story of BCDR locomotive stock was ever published and in the 1941 air raids company records in the locomotive office were destroyed by fire. Since then, much painstaking research has been done by Mr R. N. Clements and this had yielded invaluable information covering the 1847–1887 period.

In October 1846 six engine builders were asked if they could supply four locomotives within six to nine months. Sharp, Hawthorn, Forrester, Robert Stephenson, Tayleur and Bury, Curtis & Kennedy were on the shopping list, but with the railway mania at its height they had more orders on their books than they could handle. Of the six, only Bury, Curtis & Kennedy seemed likely to meet delivery, and they received the order at a price of £2,150 for each locomotive. It is probable that Bury supplied four standard 2-2-2 passenger engines, similar to those which went to the Great Southern & Western, and the Belfast & Ballymena companies about the same time. Keeping to schedule, Bury told the company on 24 June 1847 that it was ready to deliver, but the County Down was more embarassed than pleased at the news since the line to Holywood was still unfinished.

Seven 2–4–0 saddle tank engines came from Vulcan Foundry between 1864 and 1876, four of them having a temporary place in the BH&BR engine stock. This engine was first BH&BR No 3 (1876), then BCDR No 17 from 1884. It stands outside Belfast engine shed in 1905, four years before being withdrawn. (*H. Fayle*)

Manning Wardle supplied two 2–4–0 tender engines in the autumn of 1868; this photograph shows No 12, probably shortly before withdrawal in 1903. Its sister engine No 13 participated in the accident at Ballymacarrett on 13 May 1871. (*H. Fayle*)

The County Down Fowler in 1907. While this engine which was scrapped in 1909 ended its days as an 0–4–2 it is known to have been rebuilt in 1884. It is believed to have been built in 1866 by J. F. Fowler, probably as a 2–4–0T and was apparently intended for the BH&BR but was bought by the BCDR. (*H. Fayle*)

2–4–0 No 23, one of a small class of three compounds, built by Beyer Peacock in 1892. (*H. Fayle*)

Delivery was postponed until the spring of 1848, the movement of No 3 being noteworthy in that it went overboard from the ship and fell into the waters of the Liverpool dock.

The lives of these four Bury engines varied from 10 to 49 years. No 4 was sold in March 1858 to the railway contractor Moore, then building the main line south of Comber, and probably it was used on the other contracting work in County Meath. It was then repaired, and again sold, probably going to the Cork & Bandon Railway in 1867.

Nos 1 and 3 were withdrawn in 1865 and were sold to Robert Hamilton who had a timber mill in Cookstown. No 2 was modified to a 0-4-2 in the Belfast workshops of Messrs McIlwaine & Lewis and was put back into service in 1869. Heavily rebuilt in 1881, it was not withdrawn until 1897.

These standard Bury engines were unnecessarily powerful for the level Holywood traffic, and two small 2-2-2WT engines came from Messrs Fairbairn in 1850 and 1851, being officially referred to as 'No 1 Tank' and 'No 2 Tank' until the withdrawal of Bury No 4, when they were serially numbered 4 and 5. During its career No 1/4 burst four boiler tubes en route to Holywood and 'the gross neglect of Driver H. Stewart' was blamed. The County Down's engineer Domville considered a rebuild to a six-coupled engine but in the event normal boiler repair was done. Heavier trains began to tax the limited power of the Fairbairns; the first of them had a heavy overhaul and went to the Ballynahinch branch in 1871. It was withdrawn in January 1878 and sold for £237, probably going to W. J. Doherty, a contractor who used it on his Waterford Dry Dock contract. The second Fairbairn wore out more rapidly than its sister, and it was withdrawn in 1866.

These early engines were coke-burners, and that fuel was costly and in short supply in Belfast. By the 1850s the use of raw coal was being attempted by firebox modifications and success attended trials by Beattie, who was locomotive engineer on the London & South Western Railway. Beattie had the good sense to patent his invention, and he advised the Co Down engineer of the time, Firth, to obtain an engine to his specification from Beyer Peacock in Manchester. A contract for a 2-4-0T was agreed in September 1856 at £2465. It was shipped from Fleetwood to Belfast in October 1857, taking the number 5, but becoming No 7 in 1859. It was an immediate success, giving a high utilisation rate at about half the cost of the old coke-burners. A second Beattie type locomotive, No 6 came from Beyer Peacock in 1858. Both required to be reboilered after only five years, but thereafter performed well into the 1880s.

The successful debut of these two Beyers decided the purchase of a further 2-4-0T in 1858, a small engine for the Holywood traffic but apparently not a Beattie patent design, and it worked for a useful 22 years.

The line was open to Downpatrick in early 1859 and with main line goods traffic increasing, two coal-burning 0-4-2 goods engines came from Fairbairn in November 1859. More powerful than any of the earlier engines, they led Robert Gray, a director, to suggest that they be named *Samson* and *Hercules,* No 9 and No 10 on the stock list. They had various ailments, requiring new crank axles in 1862 and new boilers in 1875 and 1867 respectively. Injectors replaced water feed pumps in 1864. Both were withdrawn in 1887.

After sixteen years, the County Down had a heterogeneous stock of motive power, with 10 engines from three makers. The first approach towards standardisation came that year when the Vulcan Foundry delivered the first of a family of seven 2-4-0 saddle tanks. Their advent on the County Down was spread over 12 years; four were owned at different times by the County Down and by the Belfast, Holywood & Bangor, while three were exclusively County Down property. Around Belfast they were familiarly known as 'Badgers'; probably they would have been 'Pugs' in Scotland. Their numbering, ownership and history are summarised in the following table:

Maker's No	Delivered	1st BCDR No	BHBR No	2nd BCDR No	Renumbered	Withdrawn
508	Jan 1864	11	—	—	—	1904
537	May 1865	12	1	15	—	4/1901
538	June 1865	13	2	16	16A (1890)	7/1894
561	May 1866	3	—	—	3A (1901)	c 1903
590	Aug 1867	5	—	—	—	c 1896
793	1876	—	3	17	—	1909
197	1876	—	6	20	—	1909

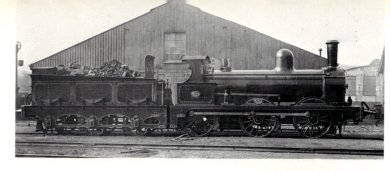

The first 0–6–0 goods engine on the County Down was this Vulcan No 14. It was delivered in July 1875 and was withdrawn in 1904 to be replaced by a second 0–6–0 of Beyer Peacock make, also No 14. (*H. Fayle*)

Of the 71 engines owned by the BCDR 42 came from Gorton Works of Beyer Peacock. This 0–6–0, No 4, was thus the first of many. It came to Belfast on 1 April 1878 and succumbed in a spate of withdrawals that followed the first world war. Its life of 44 years was punctuated by a series of derailments, the locomotive people blaming the permanent way and vice-versa. (*H. Fayle*)

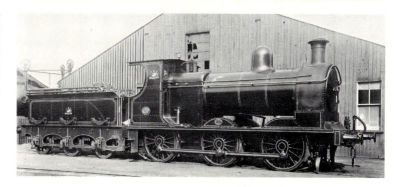

0–6–0 No 14 built by Beyer Peacock in 1904 was the first BCDR engine to have a Belpaire firebox. It is seen outside Belfast shed, resplendent with the colourful company insignia on both cabside and tender in 1907. (*H. Fayle*)

No 26 was the second Beyer Peacock 0–6–0 goods engine to come to the BCDR. It was delivered in July 1982 and worked until December 1950. (*H. Fayle*)

The Vulcan saddle tanks had a fairly varied service. Though they worked mainly to Bangor, records show that some were on the Donaghadee branch, and No 15 derailed on the way to Ardglass in 1893. No 20 features in a photograph at Downpatrick in 1900. At Knock in 1866, the new No 3 collided with Beattie No 6 which was taking an empty troop train back to town. No 16A, far from being finished, was repaired and used to ballast the Ardglass road and, since no suitable vessel could be found to ship her to the little port, she was hauled by road from Downpatrick to Killough, followed by 12 wagons in easy stages. She was feeble, and No 17 was sent to take her place.

A solitary engine was BCDR's second No 1, Fowler-built in 1866. It seems possible that its purchase was considered by the penurious BHBR,

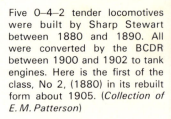

Five 0–4–2 tender locomotives were built by Sharp Stewart between 1880 and 1890. All were converted by the BCDR between 1900 and 1902 to tank engines. Here is the first of the class, No 2, (1880) in its rebuilt form about 1905. (*Collection of E. M. Patterson*)

Beyer Peacock 2–4–2T No 8 as built (1897) with short side tanks at Belfast Yard in 1917. (*H. Fayle*)

but it was paid for by the County Down. Its original wheel arrangement is not known; it may have been 2-4-0T, but it ended its days in 1909 as an 0-4-2 tender engine, following a rebuild in 1884.

Turning again from sensible standardisation, the company bought a brace of Manning-Wardle 2-4-0 tender engines in 1868. They became Nos 12 and 13 in the stock list, left vacant by the transfer of two Badgers to the BHBR. The two Manning-Wardles had a useful working life, but were criticised because of inadequate boiler capacity; after 14 years' work No 12 was given a secondhand boiler out of Fowler No 1. No 13 rose to fame by ramming a derailed engine at Ballymacarrett in May 1871; after repair it was scrapped in July 1888. No 12 broke a connecting rod in February 1890 while in the Comber cutting, destroying the piston-head and cylinder cover, but was shopped and repaired. Reboilered in 1896, it lasted until 1903 or 1904.

Unfortunately the full record of the small stock of BHBR engines is incomplete, for no records are known to exist. Critical and constructive research by R. N. Clements has replaced fiction by facts, and it is now known that the Bangor company acquired two 2-4-0 tanks, Nos 4 and 5, from Yorkshire Engine Co in 1870. Fourteen years later they came on to the County Down stock list as Nos 18 and 19 and, after overhaul, were sent to the Ballynahinch branch. They were withdrawn after seven years there, and put on reserve stock as Nos 18A and 19A. In May 1892 they were sold to a contractor for scrap after a comparatively brief working life.

A new and powerful goods engine was needed by 1874. The satisfactory history of the Vulcan Badgers led the BCDR to the Newtown-le-Willows factory for its first 0-6-0, an engine more hefty than anything that had been used before, but hard on coal. After a year it was fitted with a brick arch, which was said to have saved 10 per cent on fuel. This Vulcan served the County Down well; it was reboilered in 1895, and went on until 1904 before withdrawal.

Four years after the arrival of the Vulcan goods, another 0-6-0 was bought, but from Beyer Peacock. Its acquisition made the stock heterogeneous, but it started a trend. It came in

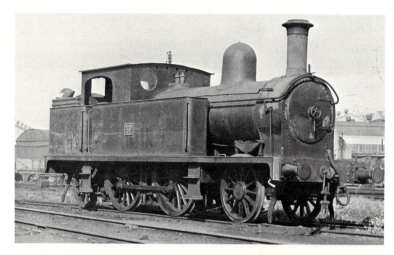

Beyer Peacock 2–4–2T No 27 built in 1897. The original short side tanks were extended in 1943. It is seen in Belfast Yard in 1950 shortly before being scrapped. (*E. M. Patterson*)

Beyer Peacock supplied the only BCDR 0–6–4T engine in 1923 and it became No 29. It was designed for shunting work in the Belfast city dock lines. With UTA roundel and numbered 229 it is seen in its final year at Queen's Quay before going to the NCC yard. (*E. M. Patterson*)

April 1878, and became BCDR's third No 4, vacated by the sale of old No 1 tank engine. Cylinder dimensions at 17in by 24in were the same as the 1874 Vulcan goods, but the wheels were an inch larger at 5ft 1in. This engine had a vigorous life span of 44 years, but achieved some notoriety because of a tendency to derail its tender. It chose the local race to do this at Downpatrick in April 1882, repeated the performance there in August 1883, and again at Belfast the next month. During the 1890s the engine derailed several times as a result of poor permanent way, and locomotive and civil engineers became involved in an exchange of vituperative comments.

After suffering six different locomotive superintendents in 32 years, stability came to Queen's Quay in the shape of R. G. Miller in 1880. He occupied his post for 39 years, only vacating it once the first world war was over. Under Miller's firm hand, the first real signs of engine standardisation became evident, though its achievement was necessarily gradual. During his first decade, five Sharp Stewart 0-4-2 mixed traffic engines with four-wheel tenders were added to stock and the fact that their working lives averaged 41 years justified their purchase. They were not above criticism and the tenders were prone to derail, especially when running tender first. As a result the entire class was rebuilt as an 0-4-2 side tank design between 1900 and 1902, in that state carrying 1000 gallons of water and $1\frac{1}{4}$ tons of coal. Parts for the conversion came from Sharp Stewart at £230–£245 a set, and labour at the County Down shops added £170 per engine to that. As tanks, the crews complained that they oscillated at high speeds, and consideration was given to lengthening the wheelbase which would have had the added advantage of giving them more bunker

Number	Date	Rebuilt	Re-numbered	With-drawn
2	1880	1902	—	1937
10	1886	1902	—	1914
9	1887	1900	28(1945)	1949
13	1888	1901	—	1921
16	1890	1901	—	1924

space. The board took advice from Bowman Malcolm of the B&NCR and his alternative suggestions of modifications to the trailing axleboxes, and a reduction of the driving wheel flanges were followed, with success.

Though John Crosthwait, Miller's successor, had decided to scrap No 9 in 1929, it was retained as a spare dock shunter and as such outlived its four sisters. In 1945 its plates were given to a new engine, and No 9 was renumbered as 28 but new plates were never actually fitted.

With still heavier trains needing more engine power, the County Down looked across the Lagan and took notice of what the Northern Counties was doing. Compound propulsion was in vogue and when in 1890 the BNCR obtained its first compounds the County Down took careful note. In August of that year, general manager Tatlow dispatched Miller to England. He went first to Gateshead to chat with Thomas Worsdell of the North Eastern, and then to Crewe to seek out Webb of the London & North Western. Miller received no encouragement at either place to use compounds on the stopping trains that characterised the County Down, and on his return informed the directors at Queen's Quay that compounds were not what was needed. But director Barbour and secretary Culverwell were enamoured of the novelty of compounding and, after argument, Miller's advice was over-ruled and he was told to obtain four 2-4-2 Worsdell von Borries compounds from Beyer Peacock. In spite of Tatlow's demand for early delivery, the County Down had to join a queue. Though Tatlow wanted them for his summer 1891 traffic, they were not delivered until the following winter, becoming Nos 18, 19, 21 and 22. They were to undergo modifications which must have taxed the County Down workshops. In their original form they had $18\frac{1}{2}$in/26in by 24in cylinders, 5ft 0in driving wheels and 4ft 0in leading and trailing wheels. Side tanks took 1150 gallons of water, and the bunkers $2\frac{1}{2}$ tons of coal. The valve gear was Walschaerts. Around 1896 the low pressure cylinders were bored out to $26\frac{1}{2}$in. Then between 1895 and 1899 all were presented with leading bogies with outside frames which put up their weight from 55 to $56\frac{1}{2}$ tons. Then, about 1897, consideration was given to making the class into simples, and No 22 was selected for conversion. Three versions were run to Bangor on trials: No 21 as a 2-4-2 compound, No 18 as a 4-4-2 compound, and No 22 as a 2-4-2 simple. The findings of the trials decided that leading bogies should be fitted to the entire class but conversion to simple expansion did not proceed further. New boilers and cylinders were fitted around 1912, and about the same year No 22 reverted to compound expansion. The diameter of the new cylinders was reduced by half an inch. All the class worked hard through the 1914–18 war, and in July 1920 they were advertised for sale in working order. No offers were forthcoming, and they were sold for scrap in 1921.

Tatlow was folloowed as general manager by Pinion, and at the December 1891 board meeting he asked his directors to sanction the purchase of two more express engines. Favourable reports of compounding continued to filter across from the Northern Counties at York Road. In the end, three Worsdell von Borries compound 2-4-0 engines were bought from Beyer Peacock, duplicates of York Road engines except for a few minor details. Cylinders were 16in/$23\frac{1}{2}$in by 24in. One of the BNCR compounds was lent for a test run to Newcastle, following which Culverwell the County Down engineer, fearing for his permanent way, registered an objection because the new engines were not to have leading bogies. In spite of Culverwell's plea, the three engines remained as 2-4-0s. They arrived in Belfast in June–July 1892, and became Nos 23, 24 and 25. By the end of the first world war they were 'well worn and in need of new boilers' and although advertised for sale in running order in April 1921 there were no takers and they went for scrap in March 1922.

With these three 1892 compounds, another 0-6-0 goods engine was ordered. Unlike its contemporaries it was a simple, with inside cylinders 17in by 24in and 5ft 1in driving wheels. It took the number 26. In its early years it suffered firebox trouble but once this was cured it coped with many years of hard work. War conditions delayed the supply of a new boiler from 1915 until 1919. Rejuvenated then, and with new cylinders, it continued to work away reliably and occasionally hauled passenger trains. It survived the grim years of a second war, its brass-rimmed splashers a reminder of more robust days. It even rolled into the grey period of Ulster Transport Authority ownership and under that regime was allocated No 226 by simple addition, but did not carry that number. It was withdrawn at the end of 1950 with over 58 years of gallant service.

Complaints were made to Beyer Peacock in the autumn of 1893 that the three new compound 2-4-0 engines, delivered in 1892, were not strong enough. The firm was asked to specify a more powerful compound engine of the same type, and also a single. It was decided to buy a simple 2-4-0, with 16in by 24in cylinders. R. G. Miller attended trials of the new engine in April 1894, and it came to Belfast in July. It became No 6, left vacant by the retirement of the 1858 Beattie. For many years No 6 was the Newcastle engine. During his first summer, John Crosthwait decided to scrap this odd engine in conformity with his policy of standardisation but there was a change of heart, No 6 was spared and entered the 1930s in excellent fettle for it was a favourite with the men. By 1941, under war conditions again, No 6 was in poor condition and seldom used. Normally it would have been cut up, but all available motive power was needed, so it was taken into the shops and given a heavy overhaul, emerging with a Belpaire boiler and firebox of the size used on the then current main-line tank engines, while 17in cylinders went in. Rebuilding lasted from August 1942 until the following March. The old engine did seven more years running before being withdrawn in January 1950 and placed in store before finally going for scrap in January 1956.

Standardisation continued when in January 1896, Beyers were given an order for a pair of 2-4-2 tank engines. Before that decision, Miller and his general manager Barber had visited Broadstone, Inchicore and Grand Canal sheds in Dublin for what might be called suburban inspiration, since the engines were mainly for work down to Bangor.

Six engines in all were ordered. They occupied the vacant numbers 5, 7 and 8, and new numbers 27, 28 and 29. The first four of the class had 16in by 24in cylinders, but Nos 28 and 29 had 17in diameter. Changes were wrought to Nos 7 and 27 in 1926/27 when their cylinders were linered down to $14\frac{1}{2}$in for use on the Holywood motor trains, thereby saving about $2\frac{1}{2}$ lb of coal per mile. The side tanks on the first four engines held 1100 gallons of water but in Nos 28 and 29 tank capacity was raised to 1300 gallons. Much later the tanks on Nos 5, 7 and 27 were reshaped to hold 1600 gallons; these three engines survived the second world war, withdrawal dates being November 1949 for the first pair, and September 1951 for No 27. Of them, R. M. Arnold wrote 'This was surely one of the merriest designs of engine ever to run in this country and any regular traveller on the Bangor line, even if he had never experienced travel himself on the "Holywood Motors" knew well that explosive sound as they shot past on the other line'.

If the County Down had a standard type of engine, within the memory of those now alive, it was represented by one of the 12 engines of a class of 4-4-2 tank. The first move in their gathering came in August 1899 when Beyer Peacock was asked for a specification and price for a pair of engines, more powerful than the 2-4-2 tanks of 1896–97. The class subdivides into three groups, with a seemingly chaotic sequence of numbers dictated by vacancies. All had 3ft 0in bogie wheels,

Beyer Peacock 4–4–2T No 19 built in 1891 as a 2–4–2T. This was one of a class of four compounds, all of which were scrapped in 1920. The class proved too rigid on curves, and the single leading axles were replaced with outside-bearing bogies. (*H. Fayle*)

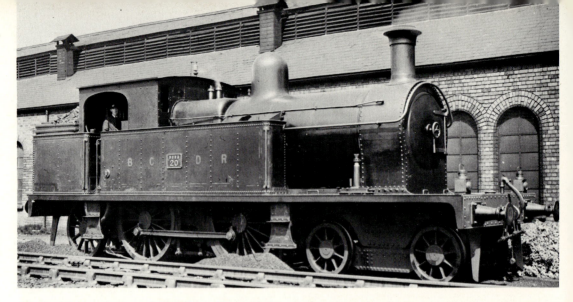

5ft 6in driving wheels and 4ft 2½in trailing wheels. The side tanks held 1600 gallons, and bunker capacity was 3 tons. The nominal weight was 55½ tons. The first group was built in 1901 and 1904, and totalled five engines, and started with round top fireboxes. The second group of three engines came in 1909 and had Belpaire boxes, with boiler centres pitched 3in above their precursors at 7ft 6in. The four engines forming the third group were built in 1921 and were practically the same as the 1909 group apart from minor differences in the boiler tubes. The first group was rebuilt between 1924 and 1931, receiving boilers and fireboxes identical with the third group but retaining the original 7ft 3in boiler line centres. A similar reboilering was afforded the engines of the second group in 1941 and 1944. Cylinder size was 17in by 24in in all cases.

These 4-4-2 tanks were most successful engines and were used over all parts of the line. The oldest, No 30, was badly damaged in a collision at Queen's Quay in 1942 and spent from June to August in the shops. It had a final heavy repair in 1949 and in February 1950 was transferred to the Northern Counties lines and based at Larne. In 1955 it returned to BCDR metals and was taken to the Transport Museum for preservation after a working life of 54 years. Other 4-4-2 tanks, of Sharp Stewart build, were common on the Dublin & South Eastern Railway but performed less actively than their Northern cousins.

The remaining 11 engines of this class were withdrawn between 1949 and 1952. No 17 spent most of its later working days running from Larne shed. All were sold for scrap in January 1956 but 11 had survived to have 200 added to their numbers by the UTA, only No 1 failing to accept that accolade since it was out of service by then.

Left: Beyer Peacock 4-4-2T No 20 in 1935. One of a class of 12 4-4-2 tank engines built between 1901 and 1921, this engine was delivered in 1909, last ran in 1951 and was scrapped in 1956. (*H. Fayle*)

Bottom left: In Ulster Transport Authority livery 4-4-2T No 208, formerly BCDR No 8 receives attention outside Belfast locomotive shed during August 1953. (*E. M. Patterson*)

Below: Rail Motor No 1 in Belfast Yard in 1907. The 0-4-0T Kitson locomotive was attached to a Metropolitan C&W coach with a total length of 63ft over the buffers. The unit lasted from 1905 to 1918. (*H. Fayle*)

The class may be summarised:

Built	BCDR Number	Maker's No
1901	30	4231
1901	3	4232
1901	15	4233
1904	11	4585
1904	12	4586
1909	1	5262
1909	17	5263
1909	20	5264
1921	13	6073
1921	18	6074
1921	19	6091
1921	21	6098

By 1903 the 1875 Vulcan goods engine was worn out, and a second 0-6-0 was needed to take its place. Surprisingly the BCDR shopped around, and tenders came from North British Locomotive Co, Vulcan, Yorkshire Engine Co and of course Beyer Peacock, which obtained the order. The new engine arrived towards the end of 1904, and occupied vacant No 14. Cylinders were 18in by 26in, driving wheels were 5ft 0in set at centres of 7ft 2in and 8ft 0in. The weight was 42 tons. For economy old Vulcan No 14's tender was utilised, with a new tank. The second No 14 was occasionally used for passenger work, though objections were raised by Arnott the civil engineer because of possible damage to his bridges, and speed restrictions were placed on its running. No 14 had its last heavy repair during 1949 and worked for a further four years before withdrawal, with scrapping following in 1954.

Two other Beyer goods engines eventually joined No 14. These were No 10 (1914) and No 4 (1921). They had similar driving wheel and cylinder sizes to the 1904 engine. They were worked hard and performed well on the Newcastle goods runs, but they were neither designed nor suited to fast passenger running to Bangor into which they were pressed from time to time.

Steam rail motors had made sporadic appearances from Inchicore on the GS&W in the 1870s, but when Dugald Drummond revitalised the idea on the LSWR in England in 1902, Nine Elms turned out the first of a series of 17 units. Various other companies followed, notably the Taff Vale and the Great Western. By 1904 the County Down was faced with the menacing prospect of a competitive roadside tramway from the city to Holywood. The directors countered swiftly and decided to acquire two rail motors for the Holywood suburban service, thereby

strangling the tramway before birth. Kitson of Leeds won the contract in August 1904 for the power units, small 0-4-0T engines which were detachable from the 56-seat carriage portion constructed by Metropolitan RC&W Co. A trial run with suitable press publicity on 29 April, went not to Holywood but to Newcastle, with the Slieve Donard Hotel as an added attraction. No sooner had the motor service began with Nos 1 and 2, than No 3 rail motor was placed on order, a larger vehicle with 16 more seats. The Kitson engine units had 10in by 16in cylinders and 3ft 7in coupled wheels. The locomotive type boilers had Belpaire fireboxes and drew water from a 400 gallon tank under the coach body. The Holywood Motors were fairly successful and they shuttled to-and-fro along the level lough shore, and also on the easily graded road as far as Dundonald. The engines were in fact stressed, and No 3 suffered a variety of mechanical troubles in the 1912–16 period. To ease its work load it was given No 1's carriage, while that engine took the heavier carriage. Poor wartime maintenance ran them into the ground and all three were unserviceable by early 1918; the power units were separated from the carriage bodies which were given new bogies and fitted for auto-train working with conventional locomotives. This practice continued until 1945, when auto-train working was abruptly ended following a serious accident at Ballymacarrett. The Kitson power units were scrapped in 1924.

Before the end of the first world war, moves were afoot among the members of the board to purchase powerful passenger locomotives. The idea was not initiated by R. G. Miller, but was forced upon that bearded patriarch by directors who had seen the Baltic tanks which had operated from 1914 on the Victoria–Brighton line of the LB&SCR. But what came to Belfast from Beyer was a sadly scaled-down version of the Brighton Baltic, with cylinders 19in by 26in instead of 21in by 28in, unsuperheated, and with driving wheels at 5ft 9in a foot smaller than the Brighton versions. The County Down Baltics had a voracious appetite for coal, and the firemen had to throw in as much as 80 pounds to the mile.

Crosthwait fell heir to four of these massive engines on his arrival and he had to make the best of them. Apart from a trial run with a stock train to Ballynahinch, they were confined to the Bangor branch and on its steep grades they produced much noise but little performance, yet they looked impressive and powerful by contrast to their lighter antecedents, and handled heavy trains with reliability rather than élan. They were numbered 22, 23, 24 and 25 (maker's numbers 5999–6002) picking up their numbers from the 2-4-0s of 1892 and a 2-4-2T of 1891. They were the only standard gauge 4-6-4 tanks in Ireland, though the Londonderry & Lough Swilly had two on its 3ft gauge line in Co Donegal.

The only 0-6-4 tank engine to work on the County Down came in 1923 from Beyer Peacock, and became the second No 29. It was designed to shunt the dock lines, where it rubbed shoulders with Great Northern engines that had come across the Central line. With driving wheels 4ft 0in in diameter, it could negotiate 170ft radius curves. Boiler and cylinders were the same as the later 4-4-2 tanks.

Left: One of the four Beyer Peacock Baltic (4–6–4) tanks which were a characteristic feature of the Bangor line from 1920. This has the UTA roundel on the cab and carries number 223 on the side tanks. With a hefty appetite for coal it is strategically placed at the Belfast coaling plant on 14 September 1950. (*E. M. Patterson*)

Below: The Harland & Wolff diesel-electric 2–4–0, seen here in July 1936 as No. D1 at Ballynahinch. (*Locomotive & General Railway Photographs*)

Belfast and County Down Railway.

Daily Cheap Fares
on
Week-days and Sundays

BETWEEN THE UNDERMENTIONED STATIONS AND **SYDENHAM** IN EACH DIRECTION.

Between SYDENHAM and		RETURN FARES.		
		1st Cl.	2nd Cl.	3rd Cl.
HOLYWOOD		9d.	7d.	5d.
MARINO		1/2	11d.	8d.
CULTRA HALT	By all Trains and Rail Motors which will permit of return same day.	1/5	1/1	9d.
CRAIGAVAD		1/7	1/2	10d.
HELEN'S BAY		2/-	1/7	1/2
CARNALEA		2/2	1/9	1/6
BANGOR WEST		2/2	1/8	1/6
BANGOR		2/2	1/8	1/6

BETWEEN THE UNDERMENTIONED STATIONS AND **HOLYWOOD** IN EACH DIRECTION.

Between HOLYWOOD and		RETURN FARES.		
		1st Cl.	2nd Cl.	3rd Cl.
SYDENHAM		9d.	7d.	5d.
MARINO		6d.	5d.	3d.
CULTRA HALT		8d.	6d.	4d.
CRAIGAVAD	Issued by all Trains and Rail Motors which will permit of return same day.	11d.	9d.	6d.
HELEN'S BAY		1/7	1/2	11d.
CARNALEA		1/9	1/6	1/2
BANGOR WEST		1/11	1/8	1/4
BANGOR		1/11	1/8	1/4

All the above Tickets are valid for Return on Day of Issue only.

BELFAST, SB/6/5/40. W. F. MINNIS, General Manager.

R. Carswell & Son, Ltd., Printers, Queen St., Belfast. (95).

The last three engines were essentially heavier versions of the 1909 4-4-2 tanks, with 18ft by 26in cylinders instead of 17in by 24in. Wheel sizes were the same, but the wheelbase was 2ft more at 29ft 3in. The boilers, water and bunker capacity were the same as the Baltics, but they were a more useful engine than the latter. Nos 8 and 16 came in 1924, No 9 followed the pair 21 years later and had the shortest life-span – 9 years – of any County Down engine. The weight of this class, 66 tons, inhibited their use beyond Comber until after 1939. During the war years No 16 was shedded at Donaghadee.

As an economy measure a 2-4-0 diesel-electric locomotive was hired in 1933 from its makers, Harland & Wolff of the great Belfast shipyard. It wore the number D1 until 1937, when it became No 2. The main dimensions were: wheels 3ft 7in, wheelbase 12ft 0in, weight $33\frac{1}{4}$ tons, engine output

Above: Baltic tank No 22 takes seven six-wheelers up the 1 in 80 bank from Holywood to Marino on 20 May 1938. (*H. S. Napier*)

Top right: 0–6–0 No 14 takes a down excursion train of eight six-wheelers past Comber up distant signal at Carnasure, one mile south of Comber, on 1 October 1932. (*W. Robb*)

Below: Wartime visitor on the BCDR. Great Southern Railways 2–4–2T No 430 at Ballynahinch Junction on 16 August 1941. (*W. Robb*)

Right: 'The Golfers' Express' between Dundrum and Newcastle headed by 4–4–2T locomotive No 18. (*Dr G. Gillespie*)

270 bhp at 850 rpm, tractive effort 8096 lb. It worked mainly on the Ballynahinch branch, and was returned to its makers in January 1952.

Harland & Wolff supplied a second diesel-electric locomotive in 1937, its type 1A–A1 and it was given the number 28. This locomotive spent most of its time on the Ardglass branch. Its weight was $48\frac{3}{4}$ tons of which $24\frac{1}{2}$ tons were adhesive. The electric motors developed 500 bhp at 800 rpm, and it had a tractive effort of 10,000 lb. It was returned to its makers in 1945, and after some service in the shipyard, later ran on the Northern Counties and Great Northern lines.

The County Down, despite its Brighton-inspired Baltic tanks, was, unlike the LBSCR, basically a suburban system, developing fairly frequent commuter workings to and from Belfast Queen's Quay. Indeed, the outstanding feature of County Down operation was the efficient working of Queen's Quay's five platforms during the morning and evening rush hours. Accurate timekeeping, both in and out, were essential.

A survey of the working timetable from 1 October 1936 shows the following 31 movements at Queen's Quay in the two hours from 07.00:

dep. 07.00 to Donaghadee
dep. 07.15 to Bangor
dep. 07.18 light engine to Comber
arr. 07.28 ex Bangor
dep. 07.30 to Donaghadee
dep. 07.33 to Bangor
dep. 07.35 to Holywood
arr. 07.38 ex Donaghadee
arr. 07.44 ex Bangor
dep. 07.45 light engine to Bangor
dep. 07.45 to Newcastle
arr. 07.48 ex Downpatrick
dep. 07.50 to Bangor
arr. 08.01 ex Holywood
dep. 08.03 to Holywood
dep. 08.05 empty coaches to Knock
arr. 08.14 ex Comber
arr. 08.18 ex Bangor
arr. 08.24 ex Holywood
dep. 08.26 to Holywood
dep. 08.29 to Bangor
dep. 08.31 to Comber
arr. 08.34 ex Bangor
arr. 08.35 ex Knock
arr. 08.40 ex Bangor
dep. 08.42 to Knock
arr. 08.42 ex Donaghadee
arr. 08.46 ex Holywood
dep. 08.50 to Holywood
arr. 08.57 ex Bangor
dep. 08.57 to Bangor

When it is realised that all these movements were routed through Ballymacarrett Junction, the pressure on the signalmen at Belfast Yard and the Junction cabins can be appreciated. All the trains, apart from the 07.15 workmen's, had three classes of accommodation, while the business trains such as the 08.20 from Bangor needed to have ample second class seats because of the popularity of the second class season or 'subscriber's' tickets. Emergency conditions after the 1941 air raids extended the activities, and the main line saw departures in the grey light of dawn: 05.20 for Donaghadee 'bread, wagons and mails', the 05.45 to Donaghadee as empty carriages with pilot engine, and the 06.10 empty stock to Saintfield to make up a departure from there at 07.00. On a Sunday night the working timetable shows a departure at 22.32 for Downpatrick as 'double train with two engines'. On the Bangor branch, a weekday train left Bangor at 05.10, to be balanced by down workings from Queen's Quay at 06.05 and 06.15, all grim evidence of shipyard workers displaced from their homes as a result of bomb damage.

Chapter 3

ROAD SERVICES

The County Down Railway was conscious that part of its territory was out of reach of its rail system, and made efforts to operate road services in those areas. In the north of Ireland, pioneering work on road services had been made at the end of the nineteenth century by the Belfast & Northern Counties Railway using steam and motor power.

Across the River Lagan the County Down Railway was not slow to follow the BNCR's example and in August 1903 began a road service down the Ards Peninsula, that finger of land to the east of Strangford Lough, from Newtownards to Portaferry and through a part of the county that had villages rather than towns. The BCDR bought a McLaren steam traction engine, with four wagons, much of whose time must have been spent in demurrage. The first ten months working lost the company £230.

It was not an encouraging start, but the company courageously bought two more steam lorries in 1904, a Leyland in January and a Londonderry in November. The Leyland was mainly occupied in hauling goods to and from Ballyherly Mill near Portaferry. The Londonderry worked along the Mourne shore between Newcastle and Kilkeel but was so unreliable that it was returned to the makers. Company records detail a succession of breakdowns and it is clear that the slow, heavy vehicles and the poor road surfaces were in mutual combat. A Mann 5 ton road lorry replaced the Londonderry in May 1905 and a somewhat uncertain service was maintained into the period of the 1914–18 war. A year after the armistice, a new Foden road motor wagon joined the fleet, and all seemed set for consolidation of the company's road freight services from other railheads. Moreover, since August 1916 the County Down had operated a passenger omnibus service between Newcastle and Kilkeel.

Once the war was over, the company found that its monopoly no longer existed and by 1922 private omnibus companies were operating out of Downpatrick and Ballynahinch; they were swiftly followed by other road freight and passenger services, not only duplicating existing services offered by rail, but duplicating each other as well. Fares were lower than those of the railway, and the public readily accepted the novelty and the convenience of a comfortable bus passing the road end. There was an excellent network of roads throughout County Down, and the County Council responded to public demand by improving road surfaces. Before long a war of fares began, a free-for-all in which the Belfast–Ballynahinch service will serve as an example of the situation. Between the two places the distance is $21\frac{1}{4}$ miles by rail and 15 miles by road. Two bus services started in July 1922, charging 2s 6d ($12\frac{1}{2}$p) for the return journey against 4s (20p) for the ordinary rail return and 2s 10d (14p) for the day rail trip, third class. To compete, the rail day trip was reduced to 2s 6d in December 1922. After some time one of the bus services was abandoned as unprofitable, then a third owner entered the field in September 1923 and worked until he became bankrupt in January 1927. During the period of this competition the bus fares were reduced to 1s 3d ($6\frac{1}{4}$p) single and 2s (10p) return, with evening trip tickets costing 1s 3d return. A fourth bus owner operated a service until his vehicle was destroyed by fire, and a fifth owner entered the fray in October 1925. Although one of the owners was unable to make the service pay when charging 2s return, a sixth owner ran a service for a time at 1s (5p) return. The rail services were further reduced in February 1928 to 8d ($3\frac{1}{2}$p) single and 1s 4d (7p) return, third class.

While the County Down Railway had been able to ensure that the Belfast, Holywood & Bangor company did not interfere with its Donaghadee traffic, it had no way of preventing road hauliers from competing, and in 1906 one Arthur Stringer introduced a summer-only horse-drawn service for passengers from Bangor to Donaghadee. Within a few years a solid-tyred charabanc run by Matthew Morrow joined the route, a pleasant run with intermittent sea views via Groomsport. The normal fare over the route was 1s (5p), but competition during the first world war became so great that at one time the fare went down to 2d (1p). Then in 1924 Morrow turned his vehicles towards the city, and his *Enterprise* buses, solid tyred, made four Bangor–Belfast runs daily, three via Clandeboye and one via Crawfordsburn, at a return fare of 1s 6d ($7\frac{1}{2}$p) while the railway's was 2s 4d (12p). The Bangor–Belfast buses were successful enough to justify a second company running in competition, and *The Bangor Queen* became a feature of the road.

Road competition also developed during the early 1920s between Bangor and Newtownards, a straight five mile road that had derived no benefit from the railway, apart from the country station at Ballygrainey two miles to the east. So two bus services opened up that area of small farms, the *Ards Transport Company* taking a direct route through the village of Conlig while *Coey's Omnibus Services* ran the dog-leg road by the Six Road Ends, where Ballygrainey station lurked. Then in 1927 the Enterprise, Bangor Queen and Ards Transport buses disappeared into the livery of the *Belfast Omnibus Company*. Two other minor bus companies centered on Bangor at that time were the *Tonic* owned by John O'Neill, and the *Pioneer* of Jacob O'Neill.

In other parts of Down, bus services began to work in competition with the railway and covered such routes as Holywood–Belfast, Kilkeel–Belfast, Ballynahinch–Dromara, Downpatrick–Strangford and Tullymurry–Ballykinler. Initially quite independent, some of these buses were persuaded to serve as feeders into and out of the rail services. However by the middle of 1927 there were no less than 27 rival bus services working against the BCDR in the county, and virtually bleeding the railway slowly to death as evidenced by the steady decline in the railway's freight and passenger receipts. The public was none the worse for it, for in the densely populated lowlands of Down, with myriad small farms, they were enjoying a far more flexible public transport service than the railway had ever provided, or ever could provide even if it had the will to do so.

The County Down Railway was slow to react positively to road competition, and it was not until May 1927 that railway-owned buses commenced rival operations. The first was a connection from the station at Donaghadee down the outer coast of the Ards peninsula to Ballywalter. Then in 1928 BCDR buses began to work on the busy road between Belfast and Holywood, already well provided for by private rivals, who were soon bought out by the railway. There is no doubt that the railway directors were slow to appreciate the public's acceptance of road buses as an alternative to the railway. The inescapable fact that in many areas the distance between urban settlements was shorter by road than by rail, gave the road buses an initial advantage and made it a practical impossibility for the railway company to recapture the traffic that it had lost. By the middle 1920s the writing was on the wall.

Chapter 4

CARRIAGES AND WAGONS

The advent of the road buses, with solid rubber tyres giving way to pneumatics after a few years, must not make us lose sight of the unforgettable six-wheeled carriages that characterised many of the trains. As speed rose on an express train descending from Craigavad to Holywood, an uninitiated passenger might well have feared the worst as the carriage pitched and hunted its terrifying way down the curving embankment, the grey sea on one side, a graveyard on the other. The unforgettable progress was accorded an orchestral accompaniment of the incessant hammering of the wheels in 1-2-3 rhythm on the rail joints and the rattling of the ill-fitting doors in their frames. For regular commuters on the 08.20 out of Bangor it was part of life.

Unfortunately little information about the early rolling stock survived the fire resulting from the air raid on 5 May 1941, but all early carriages are known to have been four-wheelers, much of them replaced in the last decade of the last century, though a few did survive until around 1914.

In the early years of the second world war coaching stock totalled 209 vehicles, made up of 18 bogie carriages, 166 six-wheelers, 9 six-wheeled passenger brake vans, 10 horse boxes, 2 carriage trucks and 4 fish vans. The County Down always offered three passenger classes. First and second class compartments had mirrors, and mounted photographs by Robert Welch of the 'Belfast and Co. Down Tourist District' above the seats, many of them rather dated landscapes which to-day would form collectors' pieces. Second and third classes were equipped with a forbidding enamelled notice reading: PLEASE DO NOT SPIT IN THE CARRIAGES. IT IS OFFENSIVE TO OTHER PASSENGERS AND IS STATED BY THE MEDICAL PROFESSION TO BE A SOURCE OF SERIOUS DISEASE. Third class compartments were comparatively spartan, with narrow five-a-side seats.

There were two early six-wheeled saloons, dating from the modernisation initiated by Tatlow. No 1 (1888) originated as a compartment first, and was a short vehicle with a wide compartment seating 10 at one end, and a saloon seating 23 at the other end. It was followed by first class No 53 in 1889, which had a central saloon flanked by small coupés. At one time it had a lavatory. For many years it worked between Belfast and Bangor, providing a card school on morning and evening trains. Two more saloons came from Ashbury in 1892 (Nos 118 and 119).

Nine six-wheeled passenger brake vans formed a series, introduced in 1890 and completed in 1902. No 9 was the last in use, eventually downgraded to delivering sacks of coal to stations on the Bangor line.

Construction of six-wheeled carriages at Belfast shops, probably about 1917. W. Napier, carriage and wagon engineer, is standing beside the half complete body of a carriage. He left the BCDR in 1919 to become locomotive engineer on the Londonderry & Lough Swilly Railway. This workshop was destroyed in the 1941 air raid. (*Courtesy H. S. Napier*)

Built at Queen's Quay in 1904, No 14 six-compartment six-wheeled second and third class composite. (*Locomotive & General Railway Photographs*)

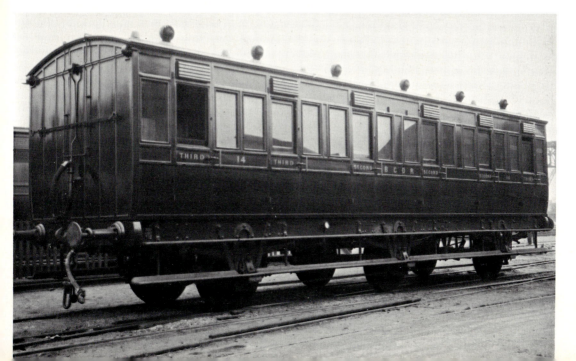

The Annual Report for 1891 records the addition of 26 passenger carriages to stock. Ten were four-compartment firsts seating 32; two became huts in Belfast yard in 1938, the rest lasted to the end of the County Down, three being converted to thirds. In the same year two brake thirds were added, the remainder of the new stock being first/second composite six-wheelers.

Bogie carriages came on the scene in 1896, when Ashbury supplied six brake thirds, with eight compartments, characteristically narrow with 5ft between partitions. Seven more followed in 1897, including four composites with a 2-1-1-1-1-2-2 layout, and two lavatory composites (Nos 150 and 152) which were used out to Donaghadee and on Belfast–Castlewellan trains. The final 1897 bogie was No 153, the splendid Royal Saloon sumptuously furnished in its initial form but later divided into a central saloon, with at one end a smoking compartment and at the other end a central corridor, flanked by washroom and wc, leading to a small non-smoking saloon. Long-stemmed gas lamps hung from the clerestory roof. This carriage had bow-ends, each with three windows. After its brief regal duty had been accomplished and up to the closure of the main line, No 153 was marshalled weekly in the Golfers' Express, leaving at noon on Saturdays. On its return from Newcastle it reassumed a familiar stance in Queen's Quay station under cover. After 1950 it had a short time working to Bangor, then went to the Northern Counties section until it was sold in 1954.

The most numerous type of carriage was the six-compartment second class six-wheeler. There were 41 in all, built at Queen's Quay shops between 1905 and 1920. About a third of them had electric light, the others were gas-lit. One was destroyed in the air raid, another was badly damaged in the 1945 Ballymacarrett accident and was not repaired.

The last six-wheelers were built in 1923, but in the previous year the County Down bought some second-hand Great Northern six-wheeled thirds.

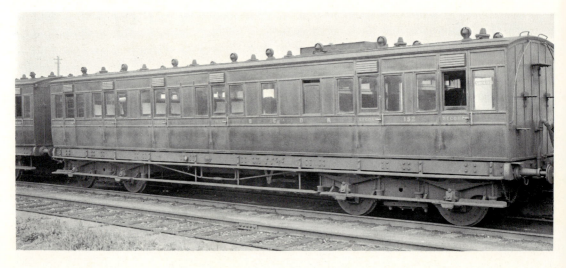

No 108 six-wheeled third class carriage built in 1886. Alternate compartments had low seat backs dividing the coach into three pairs of compartments with each pair sharing a lamp and roof ventilators. (*Locomotive & General Railway Photographs*)

In 1928 eight more obsolescent six-wheelers came from the Northern Counties to replace the old GN stock, and 10 years later two were wrecked when they were shunted into the buffers at Bangor. These NCC vehicles were conspicuous by their inherited large digit '3' on the doors, the County Down preferring to put the class in letters.

From 1928 to 1938 money was short and the status quo prevailed. Then in 1938 two new bogie tri-composites (Nos 120, 121) were bought from Pickering of Wishaw, the arrangement being 2-2-2-1-1-2-2-3-3. Smooth running and relatively quiet they were undoubtedly the most 'luxurious' carriages ever to run on County Down rails. A wartime request to the government for a licence to buy two more from Pickering was refused.

Final additions to stock came in 1943 in the form of four six-wheeled bogie composites of varying make-up from Northern Counties stock, via a reconditioning visit to the Great Northern's Dundalk shops. They formed one set on the Bangor line.

Remaining passenger stock included six horseboxes, four of which were four-wheeled and two six-wheeled. Originally numbered 1–10 in their own list, renumbering in 1945 brought them into the main list as Nos 191–200. There were also four six-wheeled ventilated vans, built for Ardglass fish traffic but latterly used for bread. They were moved to NCC metals after 1950. Finally there were the two carriage trucks and an elderly six-wheeled breakdown van.

Carriage livery was crimson lake, lined in either yellow ochre or straw. The coach ends and headstocks were crimson, the solebars and ironwork was black. After 1945 coach ends began to be painted black. The initials 'BCDR' and the vehicle number were carried at waist level once on each side. Block letters were normal, but in the 1920s some Old English capitals appeared on second/third composites. Under the UTA from 1 October 1948, an eight-coach train of bogies came from the NCC in crimson lake livery. Then in early 1949, brunswick-green UTA livery began to replace the familiar lake.

During 1950 all BCDR straight-sided six-wheeled carriages went to the NCC for excursion trains, and in replacement more ex NCC bogie stock appeared on the Bangor line, where they were joined by an ex-English Midland first, later altered to a first/second composite. In the following year old ex-BNCR stock with straight sides was drafted in, and most of the more modern carriages went back to the Northern Counties section. Dieselisation then began.

As regards wagon stock it must be remembered that goods traffic did not account for more than a fraction of the company's receipts. Accordingly goods and departmental vehicles are less numerous and less complex in their history than other Irish companies. In the beginning the company had no wagons, for there was no goods service to Holywood. For the opening to Newtownards three cattle wagons, two covered wagons, three open wagons and four stone wagons were bought from Thomas Firth, a Belfast coachbuilder. From the great quarries along the eastern face of Scrabo Hill above Newtownards, stone traffic developed rapidly since wrought sandstone blocks were in great demand to build the expanding city. Within eight years 30 stone wagons were in use. Five covered wagons and two passenger brake vans came from Dickson of Wellington, Salop.

With extension of the main line, the wagon stock was increased and in January 1857 70 wagons were ordered from Dawson & Sons of Dublin. The limited workshop capacity was already busy with repair work but, in mid-1859, it was decided to build wagons at Queen's Quay in addition to those bought in from a variety of cross-channel sources (Olbury, Metropolitan and Midland). By 1875 the stock total was 308, when the trauma of the change of Board occurred. At that time many wagons were decrepit, and about one in seven was in the workshops either being repaired or awaiting attention. Under the new and more vigorous management worn out vehicles were scrapped and new orders placed. By the time the BHBR was acquired in 1884 the stock total was 335, not including five goods brakes in a separately numbered series.

Berkeley Wise, the County Down civil engineer from 1877 to 1888, demanded his own ballast

One of the two bogie lavatory composite carriages, No 152, used on Donaghadee line trains. Two of the three first class compartments in the centre and the two second class compartments nearest the camera had access respectively to one of the two toilet compartments. (*Locomotive & General Railway Photographs*)

wagons but, denied new vehicles, had to be content with 29 secondhand ones from the Londonderry & Lough Swilly Railway when that company regauged its Buncrana line from 5ft 3in to 3ft 0in. He got ten ballast wagons at the auction for £5 12s 6d (£5.62½) each, obviously in poor condition. Culverwell followed Wise in office, and secured permission to buy a dozen 16 ton, six-wheeled open wagons for ballast working, which were built by the BNCR at York Road in 1890. One of them, albeit rebuilt, passed into UTA stock in 1948.

Under the guidance of Joseph Tatlow as general manager an intensive programme of construction of standard 8 ton open wagons was launched. Outside tenders were too high, so the Queen's Quay shops tackled the work. Many were rebuilt to 10 tonners, which later became the standard. In 1891 the stock was augmented by 25 opens from Queen's Quay, plus 50 from Metropolitan.

From 1890 onwards large numbers of a standard side-door 10 ton wagons were added to stock; some were built by the company, but Metropolitan and Hurst Nelston were also builders. They had four-plank sides, compared to the earlier three-plank 8 tonners.

Goods and cattle wagons originally had an open centre section in the roof which was covered as required by a tarpaulin. Goods brake vans, totalling 12 in 1912, were outside framed with double doors, side pillars and a small end compartment for the guard with handbrake, seats and a stove.

There were three vehicles which were not classified in the six-monthly returns up to 1912. One was the weighbridge van, and the others were two gasholder trucks, which conveyed oil-gas under pressure from the manufacturing plant at Belfast to Ballynahinch and Downpatrick respectively, where the gas-lit branch carriages' reservoirs were replenished. Carriage lighting by compressed oil-gas was introduced in 1893, before which Colza-oil lamps were in use.

With a backlog of repairs on hand at the end of the first world war, plans were made for a vigorous programme of workshop effort. But these plans had to be changed and by 1924 road competition was causing goods traffic to fall away and in consequence spending on the wagon shop had to be greatly reduced. By 1931 the mechanical engineer John Crosthwait found himself with 66 wagons on the condemned list and 196 more awaiting repairs. The 1930s were indeed years of poverty.

The second world war reversed the company's decayed fortunes when fresh traffic returned from the roads, and the Queen's Quay shops were again busy on repairs and rebuilds. When the County Down handed over operations to the Ulster Transport Authority three years after the end of war, the UTA inherited 629 traffic and 77 departmental wagons. Of the former, 77 needed repair. The total comprised:

Traffic

Goods and cattle	119
Covered goods	174
Open, side door, 10t	229
Open, side door, 8t	35
Open, dropside, 8t	53
Open, box, 8t	1
Timber trucks, 10t	3

Timber truck runner	1
Brake vans, 12t	5
Brake vans, 7t	9
Departmental	
Ballast drop-side	23
Rail 12t	9
Ballast brake	1
Loco coal	38
Loco ash	2
Gasholder trucks	2
Breakdown van	1
Weighbridge van	1

Of the goods and cattle wagons 45 were vacuum braked, 34 were piped and could run in passenger trains. Two of the covered goods were vacuum fitted. Four covered goods were kept for yarn traffic to Messrs Andrews Mill at Comber, two were for meat and six were for tar, but all were in general use prior to 1948.

Though grease-filled axle boxes were standard on wagons, oil boxes were used on vacuum fitted and piped vehicles, on brake vans and on the rail wagons. Livery was dark grey, but red oxide was applied to pw department wagons and to fitted and piped stock. During the two years between the UTA takeover and the 1950 closures, many wagons were moved over to the NCC, and were listed there, 6000 being added to their County Down numbers. A similar renumbering was applied to the wagons that remained at Queen's Quay.

Under UTA ownership some fitted cattle wagons were repainted green, while some piped wagons became NCC light grey. Permanent way vehicles began to appear in red oxide and grey. Shortly afterwards, in conformity with plans to discontinue rail goods traffic, the UTA ceased to paint wagons and any replacement timbers were preserved with clear cuprinol, which gave repaired wagons an unusual appearance. Thus scattered over a declining network of UTA lines, County Down wagons went far afield but their numbers were soon reduced by a series of rolling stock auctions in the 1950s and 1960s.

Above left: Ballynahinch station on 4 July 1936, with the diesel-hauled branch train on the right, goods wagons stabled in the station, and wagons being unloaded on the left. Notice the sheeted open roof sections in the otherwise covered vans. (*Locomotive & General Railway Photographs*)

Below: At Ballygowan, 4–4–2 tank No 20 halts with the 7 pm Newcastle–Belfast on 4 July 1933. The train is a mixture of bogie and six-wheeled stock. (*W. Robb*)

Chapter 5

TWO MAJOR ACCIDENTS

The County Down Railway only suffered two serious accidents in its lifetime, both of which took place in the vicinity of Ballymacarrett Junction, just outside Queen's Quay. When the first occurred, on 13 March 1871, the BCDR and the BHBR were operating two separate establishments at Queen's Quay and the single lines of the two ran parallel for about half a mile to their divergence at Ballymacarrett which, at that time, was not a junction. The accident involved two trains and took the form of a collision. The 8.30pm down goods was being made up in the yard and the engine (No 5 Vulcan 2-4-0ST with Driver Spence and Fireman Trainor) had gone to the water column. Spence climbed on to the tank, leaving Trainor on the footplate. Both had 'drink taken'. Somehow Trainor broke the handle of the injector. The driver again left the fireman in charge and went to obtain a substitute handle, having en route to get a key to the workshop, at the time office. On his way to the shops with the key he noticed that the train was on the move, but continued on his way and, when he came out, saw that No 5 and its wagons had stopped some way along a long headshunt. In fact No 5 was off the road and was fouling the main line. An up train was due. Trainor realised too late the error of his ways, but instead of running down the main line and attempting to stop the oncoming train, he panicked and ran towards the terminus, ostensibly to inform the foreman. The up train, headed by Manning Wardle No 13 in the charge of Driver Lyons and Fireman Green had no warning, rounded the curve and collided with the obstruction. Two passengers were killed. Fireman Trainor in fact never reached the shed, but left the railway premises and was found some time later by the police 'drunk and asleep' in his home at Bridge End. He was tried in July on a charge of manslaughter, found guilty and sentenced to 12 months hard labour.

The second accident was much more serious and occurred during the blackout of the second world war, a short way down the Bangor branch from the junction. In darkness and fog at about 07.50 on 10 January 1945, between Victoria Park Halt and the junction station, the 07.40 push-and-pull, or motor train from Holywood ran into the rear of the 07.10 passenger train from Bangor. The motor train consisted of bogie control carriage and two six-wheel carriages propelled by 2-4-2T No 5, running bunker first. The Bangor train was made up of 13 six-wheel carriages hauled by 4-6-4T No 25, and had been halted at Ballymacarrett

Left: During 1945 when a heavy goods train of 13 vehicles got away on the down grade into Bangor the engine demolished the buffers and concourse railing. The crew have thrown the fire out and staff from Queen's Quay are debating how to rerail unlucky No 13. *(P. Megraw)*

Above: Ballymacarrett 13 May 1871: the scene after the accident. *(R. J. Welch, courtesy Ulster Museum)*

Below: The terrible aftermath of the accident that occurred on 10 January 1945 between Victoria Park Halt and Ballymacarrett Junction. The GN breakdown crane is lifting the BCDR motor train bogie carriage clear of the wreckage of six wheeled carriage No 9, whose body was totally destroyed in the collision; 23 people were killed and 41 injured. *(Courtesy Ulster Museum)*

Junction home signal. The Holywood rail motor had already been stopped at the Sydenham automatic stop signal and under the rules had waited for two minutes before proceeding with caution to Victoria Park Halt, where it stopped in thickening fog to set down passengers. It then ran on towards the junction, passing Ballymacarrett distant signal which was at caution. About 30yd away the red tail-light of the stationary Bangor train loomed up through the murk. The heavy leading coach of the motor train, impelled by the engine at the rear, collided violently with the rear of the crowded Bangor train. The leading coach mounted the underframe of second/third class composite No 9, completely destroying it and went on to penetrate for a distance of 10ft, the bodywork of second class carriage No 22. In those last pair of carriages, 23 passengers were killed and 41 injured. Damage to the heavy bogie control carriage was comparatively light, and the track was quite undamaged. The County Down practice of 'stop and proceed' working in which trains halted at automatic stop signals for two minutes (four in fog or falling snow) and was then permitted to proceed, plus the fact that the driver was neither required nor able (in the absence of such facilities) to telephone the signalman was a dangerous procedure. The speed of progression from signal to signal was left to the driver's judgment. On 10 January 1945 the potentially dangerous position was compounded by there being several unauthorised passengers in the driving cab. Various changes in working procedure were at once introduced, telephones were fitted at signals, and no more motor trains were run. Compensation paid by the company to victims and dependants amounted to £75,000, the loss of such a massive sum of money adding further to the financial burden that the company faced now that peacetime working was approaching.

Chapter 6

UNDER THE ULSTER TRANSPORT AUTHORITY

During 1946, with the horror of the Ballymacarrett accident still in peoples' minds, the Government made public its intention of bringing together under one public management the Northern Ireland Road Transport Board, the BCDR, the LMS(NCC) and the GNR(I). The body thus created would have full control and responsibility for all internal public transport in Northern Ireland. The proposals were published as a Bill in 1947 and were implemented in 1948 by the Transport Act (NI) although the cross-border system of the GNR(I) introduced complex political and administrative problems which were not finally sorted out for another decade or more. On 30 September 1948 the independent life of the County Down Railway was extinguished and it became a part of the Ulster Transport Authority. It was six weeks plus a century after the opening of the Belfast–Holywood branch.

Compensation offered to the County Down shareholders for the UTA take-over was £485,990, a sum which immediately provoked criticism, shareholders declaring that the line was worth at least £1,175,000, while a certain Stormont MP remarked that since the railway could not run at a profit it had no saleable value at all.

Under the UTA the County Down system continued to operate, much as before, for $15\frac{1}{2}$ months. The travelling public saw NCC bogie coaches replace the old six-wheelers on the Bangor section, and some goods wagons became green. In early 1949 it was announced that it was proposed to close the entire County Down system apart from the Bangor branch and the Castlewellan–Newcastle spur, which the Great Northern used. From 7 March 1949 the timetable showed drastic reductions in services. A Sunday train no longer ran to Donaghadee, and the main line had one train in each direction. Steam traction continued, and the boiler of old No 6 was retubed and that 2-4-0 sent to Newcastle shed from where it handled the down Golfers Express on Saturdays. On the Bangor branch, four NCC Class W Moguls that had been repaired at Harland & Wolff's shipyard appeared, running-in before returning to their parent line. They were unable to turn, and worked tender-first in one direction. They were followed by NCC Class WT 2-6-4 tanks.

In that Indian summer of 1949, workings on the Bangor branch were full of interest and the smart performance of the 2-6-4 tanks derived in effect from their British Fowler/Stanier counterparts on the LMS was in contrast with the proverbially sluggish County Down Baltics. The end seemed far away. On one Saturday there were two livestock specials from Downpatrick to Belfast, two Sunday School specials from Newtownards to Newcastle, and three excursions off the Great Northern and over the Central to Bangor. Then from 24 October 1949 the winter timetable carried forebodings of the end. The Transport Tribunal's findings were announced in December, and the UTA gave notice of the first closures: all services south of Comber were to cease after 15 January 1950. On that final Sunday the main line was busy, the normal trains ran but empty stock was worked back to Belfast. From the Ballynahinch branch diesel No 2 and its two carriages worked gently down to Newcastle, to commence a local service to Castlewellan the following day since the UTA had found it was legally bound to work the old County Down's share, so long as Great Northern trains were on it. The last up train left Newcastle shortly after 19.00, double-headed by 0-6-0 No 14 and 4-4-2T No 21. Northwards they went through the winter darkness and at every station on the road exploding volleys of detonators echoed in sad salute.

For some odd reason the Belfast–Comber–Donaghadee section survived until 22 April 1950, and at the same time the UTA's Castlewellan service came to an end, the diesel train returning slowly over the rusted main line the next day. With Queen's Quay sidings cluttered with stock, trains of carriages were taken over to the NCC and parked in such unlikely places as Aghadowey on the deserted Derry Central line.

The postscript to the foregoing falls into three parts, the first two parts lasting respectively 15 and 11 years, the third is still in progress. The remnant

Two BCDR 4–4–2 tanks, in UTA livery, cross at the down end of Newtownards station. No 212 brings in the morning Donaghadee goods while No 219 approaches with a passenger train from Donaghadee in December 1949. (*E. M. Patterson*)

of the BCDR, the Bangor branch, remained connected with the rest of Ireland's railways from 1950 until mid-1965, thereby constituting the first part of the postscript.

On 31 July 1965 the Central line was severed when its bridge over Middlepath Street was removed in connection with road improvements. This introduced the second phase of the postscript, and isolated the Bangor section, in some ways reducing it to the status of the Waterford & Tramore section in the south of the Republic. This phase lasted for almost 11 years.

The final phase dates from the reopening of the Central section, reconnecting the Bangor branch with the rest of the country, and enabling through timetable working to begin from Bangor to Lisburn and Portadown on the former Great Northern system.

From 1950 until 1953 steam hauled trains characterised the Bangor line. Diesel multiple-units were introduced during 1953, and by mid-June nine three-car sets were at work maintaining 85 per cent of the mileage. The remainder of the services were worked by NCC 2-6-4 tank engines and occasionally by BCDR 4-4-2T No 217. From 26 November 1953 the whole of the Bangor service was run by multi-engined diesel sets. The sidings at Queen's Quay gathered a bizarre and decaying line of once-familiar County Down engines, awaiting their fate.

Those engines lay in the sidings for two years in some cases, until on 19 January 1956 came the first of two auctions, when three of the Baltics Nos 223–5, the three large 4-4-2 tanks Nos 208/9/16, 11 of the small 4-4-2 tanks Nos 201/3, 211–3/5/7–21, a couple of goods engines Nos 204 and 210, and the solitary, big-wheeled 2-4-0 No 206 were sold for scrap. There survived a solitary Baltic, working across on the NCC, and the dock shunter No 229 which had also been translated across the river. No 230 was in store awaiting transfer to the Transport Museum. The second auction on 29 June 1956 saw Nos 222 and 229 go.

During 1956 minor modifications took place to the diesel railcars on the Bangor line. For three years the section had been operated by 14 three-car sets, a total of 42 vehicles of which 28 were power cars with 125hp engines. At peak times they were marshalled into six-car sets, each with four power cars. During the year they were gradually re-engined with 165hp motors, the extra power enabling them to be worked as four-car sets, with power cars at each end.

The viability of some stations fell under the eye of management and since Kinnegar, Marino, Cultra and Craigavad had comparatively light traffic, they were closed on 11 November 1957. Public demand resulted in the reopening on 4 January 1960 of Marino and Craigavad, but the latter was again closed on 12 June 1961. The station buildings remained in existence, and the stationmasters' houses were rented as private residences. During 1961 single power cars were put into use on off-peak trains to Bangor, and Nos

24, 26 and 28 were provided with controls in the guard's compartment. During 1961, in the month of February, the Central's viaduct over the River Lagan was hit by a coal barge and had to be closed for 10 days for repairs.

On the Central line, economies were made during 1964 when the entire section was made single track and the signal cabins at Maysfields and East Bridge Street were abolished, the section being worked by tablet and telephone. The points at Maysfields and Gas Works sidings were operated by ground frame. In November 1964 first class travel was ended on the Bangor line diesel sets, the original second class having been merged with third class a decade earlier, and later called second class.

With the steady increase in the number of private cars commuting into the city, road traffic congestion had become acute by the early 1960s, and it was decided to construct a new river bridge to try to relieve pressure on the old Queen's and Albert Bridges. This new bridge was made immediately down-river from the Queen's Bridge, and a broad road was driven from its eastern end through decaying property to connect with the existing Sydenham By-Pass road, its construction involving the removal of the Middlepath Street railway bridge. This was carried out on 31 July 1965, effectively isolating the Bangor branch completely and preventing access to it by occasional excursion trains. Dock traffic had already disappeared. Queen's Quay station

Ballynahinch Junction on 3 January 1950. The six-wheelers of the 10.45 am Newcastle have arrived from Belfast and are met by the Ballynahinch branch train headed by Harland & Wolff diesel-electric locomotive No 2 (formerly No D1). (*E. M. Patterson*)

remained as before, a vast anachronistic edifice, with four platforms remaining out of the original five. The convenient tramcar bay was merely a memory, and city buses stopping by the portico were a poor substitute.

About this time the railcars on the County Down section were given a new distinctive livery of cream on olive-green, while other distinctive liveries were bestowed on railcars on the old GN and NCC sections. A standard maroon and grey livery followed a year later.

Also during 1965 a new compact signal cabin was built outside Queen's Quay station, eventually taking over in June 1966 the duties of the large Belfast Yard cabin, and the smaller Ballymacarrett Junction cabin both of which had become irrelevant. At around the same time the UTA felt that hotel management was not for them, and sold its six station hotels, including the Slieve Donard which was by then 10 years away from sight and sound of a train.

Back on the Bangor line, two new halts were needed: Crawfordsburn Hospital halt between Carnalea and Helen's Bay, serving the former Crawfordsburn House was opened on 31 September 1965, and on 4 April 1966 Seahill was opened between Helen's Bay and Craigavad where a small new town had grown between the main road and the coast. In the 1930s a planned town was to have been sited there, named Port Kennedy, but had been inhibited by the war.

The great increase in the commuter private cars into Belfast has been mentioned. By the late 1960s Holywood was forming a pronounced bottleneck, and mile-long queues of slow-moving cars were a feature of morning and evening traffic there. The position was becoming intolerable, if only for the folk who lived in Holywood, and the Government decided to by-pass the town by a road alongside the railway. On the climb between Holywood and Marino it was necessary to resite the railway embankment a short way out to sea. The scheme was publicised in mid-1967 but work did not commence until 1 May 1970, the new section of line coming into use on 28 March 1971.

Meanwhile, the UTA, a nationalised undertaking, was accused by many as having an anti-rail bias. Its chairman, one John Coulthard who had long experience in railway operating matters, was dismissed his post on 8 May 1967 and a storm of protest resulted, including a short strike by railwaymen. He was replaced as chief executive by Hugh Waring, who had joined the County Down Railway as a porter at the age of 14, was later a full-time official of the National Association of Transport Employees and in 1964 became personnel officer of the UTA and then manager of the central area of Ulsterbus Ltd.

Chapter 7
ULSTER TRANSPORT AUTHORITY TO NORTHERN IRELAND RAILWAYS

A new Transport Bill, published on 19 August 1967 completed the legislative proposals announced by the Northern Ireland Government in 1964. The measures were to reorganise the UTA into specialised operating units for railway, for road passenger and for road freight. The UTA was to be wound up and its assets and responsibilities transferred to a Holding Company. The duty to operate rail services was to be transferred to a separate undertaking to be named Northern Ireland Railways Company Ltd, a wholly owned subsidiary of the proposed Holding company. On 1 April 1968, perhaps an inauspicious date, the Bill became law and NIR came officially into being. It was divided into four 'regions', the Bangor line being the sole component of the Down Region.

During the early part of 1970 the Northern Ireland Ministry of Development announced a Ten Year Plan for NIR which included the restoration of the Belfast Central line as double track, and with it the reconnection of the Bangor line. Matters moved slowly and two years were to pass before any action was visible to the public.

With only the Bangor branch remaining, the UTA brought across some of the Midland engines from York Road. Here is an immaculately clean 2–6–4T No 7 at platform 3 of Queen's Quay terminus preparing to take out a Bangor train in August 1953. (*E. M. Patterson*)

Meanwhile Northern Ireland had begun to experience the rigours of a terrorist campaign, skilfully orchestrated and verging on guerilla war. Public utilities were to suffer innumerable acts of sabotage, the railways bearing their share. The former Great Northern suffered most by reason of its geographical position, but the surviving remnant of the County Down soon felt the impact. To name only a few incidents, on 27 November 1971 a terrorist bomb exploded in Queen's Quay station, causing considerable damage to the concourse and its glass roof. In October 1973 a bomb exploded on the 12.20 down train at Marino, badly damaging multi-engined diesel trailer 526 and railcars 15 and 16.

On 10 February 1972 it was announced that the Northern Ireland Government had accepted plans for the construction of a new Central Station on the old Central line at the site of the Great Northern cattle depot, to the south of East Bridge Street, and the reconstruction of the Central line from the Great Northern end at Central Junction to the County Down end at Ballymacarrett Junction. A new station was to be built at Botanic Avenue. The Lagan viaduct, by then colloquially known as the Shaky Bridge, was to be demolished and replaced by a modern twin-track river crossing. In October 1973 the contract for the renovations was let to Messrs Graham of Dromore.

Work proceeded through 1974 and 1975, new roads being built to give unrestricted bus access to the Central Station. On the Bangor line the footbridge at Kinnegar Halt was removed, and at five other overbridges the track formation was lowered to give adequate clearance for the eventual passage of diesel-electric locomotives. The old BHBR sandstone viaduct over Crawfordsburn Glen, widened at the doubling of the line by metal outriggers, was completely redecked over many weekends. The old Queen's Quay workshops were refurbished to provide central servicing facilities for railcars and motive power, thus replacing the GN shops at Adelaide. The automatic banner semaphore signals were replaced by colour lights. Queen's Quay station remained in use as before, but once the Central line was connected it would become redundant, as would the Great Northern terminus at Great Victoria Street.

On 10 April 1976 work on the Central line was practically complete, and when the last train had left for Bangor, Queen's Quay was closed and the following morning Bangor trains ran into Central station. Great Victoria Street station continued to function for a fortnight, then it was closed on 24 April 1976. On the last day of service, passenger trains out of Great Victoria Street were worked along the 'third road' and through Adelaide freight yard, while the Central line was being connected to Great Northern metals.

Thus after a period of limbo that had lasted just over $11\frac{1}{4}$ years, the Bangor line, inbred to the sight and sound of an ageing multi-engined diesel railcar fleet, had its renaissance. The 128-year old concept of a terminus at Queen's Quay vanished overnight, and rolling stock and motive power from other parts or Ireland was free to run on to the surviving fragment of the County Down.

At the time there were, broadly speaking, three classes of diesel railcars at work on NIR. There were the old MED (multi-engined) diesel units, the

Left: An early multi-engined diesel (MED) train set with Nos 10 and 11 power cars entering Bangor West Halt from Bangor on 1 September 1952. These Units were unique in the British Isles in having power sliding doors. *(E. M. Patterson)*

Below: An excursion train of ex-GN bogie stock headed by ex-GNR 0–6–0 No 48 of UTA drifts through Bangor West Halt on a summer afternoon in 1961. The sandstone overbridge has been disfigured by a water pipe. *(E. M. Patterson)*

later BUT railcars that the GN had fostered, and the newer MPD (multi-purpose diesel) which York Road had developed as a cheap substitute for locomotive haulage of light freight trains.

In 1966 the first of a fleet of diesel-electric railcars had been introduced, starting with the class 70 (Nos 71–78). These were followed in 1974 by the similar class 80 (Nos 82–89, 90–99 and then a backspill of numbers to 67–69). These ran basically as three-car sets with a power car, an intermediate coach, and a driving trailer. They were worked first on the NCC line, but once the Central connection had been established, they were brought on to the Bangor line, and now operate all timetabled traffic in and out of Bangor. The MED railcars were progressively withdrawn and scrapped, the last in 1980, and all BUT cars have now gone. The disposal of both classes presented unforseen problems, due to the health hazard of blue asbestos insulation, and the majority were drowned in a flooded quarry near Crumlin. BUT and MPD railcars were not seen in regular service to Bangor, but occasionally visited the line on excursion traffic. Similar occasional visits are paid by units of NIR's small team of diesel-electric locomotives, hauling ordinary coaches. These locomotives are currently the three 1350hp Hunslet Bo-Bos (Nos 101, 102 and 103) and two 2250hp General Motors types. There are also three diesel-hydraulic locomotives (Nos 1, 2, 3) which work permanent way trains over the whole NIR system and occasionally are to be seen on the Bangor line.

Passenger workings out of Bangor work to Portadown, to Lisburn or to Central, with balancing workings in the down direction. With hindsight it is interesting to speculate how operating methods to-day might differ had the axe been spared on the main County Down line out as far as Comber, where the recent suburban expansion would have guaranteed a substantial commuter traffic. Certainly on the Bangor line, the terminus might justifiably exhibit a phoenix in juxtaposition to the NIR logo.

BIBLIOGRAPHY

Fayle, H. (1906) 'The Belfast and County Down Railway'. *Railway Magazine, 18,* 356, 494

Gentry, W. C. (1913) 'The Belfast and County Down Railway'. *Railway & Travel Monthly, 6,* 458

Tatlow, J. (1920) *Fifty Years of Railway Life.* London

Lee, C. E. (1939) 'The Belfast and County Down Railway'. *Railway Magazine, 84,* 346

Reed, K. H. (1939) 'Locomotives of the B & CDR. *Railway Magazine, 84,* 416

Fayle, H. (1941–42) 'The Belfast & Co. Down Railway and its Locomotives'. *The Locomotive Magazine, 47,* 215, 262; *48,* 12, 37

Coakham, D. G. (1950) 'The County Down Area of the Ulster Transport Authority'. *Journal of the Stephenson Locomotive Society, 26,* 110

Patterson, E. M. (1950) 'The Last Days of the County Down'. *Meccano Magazine, 35,* 201

Patterson, E. M. (1953) 'Steam-Diesel Transition in Ulster'. *Meccano Magazine, 38,* 252

Patterson, E. M. (1953) 'The Belfast-Bangor Line in 1953'. *Trains Illustrated, 6,* 219

Hodge, A. T. (1954) 'Railways at Belfast'. *Railway Magazine, 100,* 682

Arnold, R. M. (1955) 'The Belfast & County Down Railway, its decline and fall'. *Journal of the Irish Railway Record Society, 4,* 1

Patterson, E. M. (1958) *The Belfast & County Down Railway.* Oakwood Press

Coakham, D. G. (1965) 'Passenger Stock of the B & CDR'. *Journal of the Irish Railway Record Society, 7,* 176

Clements, R. N. (1967) 'Beyer Engines in Ireland'. *Journal of the Irish Railway Record Society, 8,* 42

Robb, W. (1967) 'Recollections of the B & CDR'. *Journal of the Irish Railway Record Society, 8,* 30

Arnold, R. M. (1969) *Steam over Belfast Lough.* Oakwood Press

Baker, M. H. C. (1972) *Irish Railways since 1916.* Ian Allan Ltd.

Coakham, D. G. (1972) 'The Ballymacarrett Accident' *Journal of the Irish Railway Record Society, 10,* 159.

Coakham, D. G. (1973) 'B & CDR Wagon Stock'. *Journal of the Irish Railway Record Society, 11,* 16

Coakham, D. G. (1975) 'Private Owners' Wagons, B & CDR'. *Journal of the Irish Railway Record Society, 12,* 151

Gamble, N. E. (1976) 'Belfast Central'. *Journal of the Irish Railway Record Society, 12,* 257

Robb, W. (1978) 'Decline and Revival in Northern Ireland'. *Journal of the Irish Railway Record Society, 12,* 218

Gamble, N. E. (1978) 'N.I.R. Railcars: a brief survey, I': *Journal of the Irish Railway Record Society, 13,* 236

Arnold, R. M. (1981) *The County Down.* Irish Steam Scene. Whitehead

APPENDIX

LIST OF STATIONS AND HALTS

	Open	Closed	Distance from Queen's Quay		R.C.H. Classification (see below)
Bangor Branch			miles	chains	
Belfast (Queen's Quay)	1848	1976	—	—	GPLHC (4)
Ballmacarrett	1905	1977	0	71	—
Victoria Park	1905	—	1	24	—
Sydenham	1851	—	1	70	P
Glenmachan	1863	?	2	20	—
Tillysburn	1848	1945	2	53	P
Kinnegar	1905	1957	3	64	—
Holywood	1848	—	4	37	GPLHC
Marino	{ 1870 1960	1957 —	5	27	P
Cultra	1865	1957	6	03	P

Station	Opened	Closed	Miles	Chains	Facilities
Craigavad	1865 / 1960	1957 / 1961	6	45	GP
Seahill	1966	—	7	57	—
Clandeboye, *later* Helen's Bay	1865	—	9	00	GPC
Crawfordsburn Hospital	1965	—	9	63	—
Carnalea	1873(?)	—	10	40	P
Bangor West	1928	—	11	20	—
Bangor	1865	—	12	20	GPLHC (2)

Main Line

Station	Opened	Closed	Miles	Chains	Facilities
Fraser Street	1930	1950	0	45	—
Bloomfield	1879	1950	1	40	P
Neill's Hill	1890	1950	2	25	P
Knock	1850	1950	2	60	P
Dundonald	1850	1950	4	78	GP
Comber	1850	1950	8	00	GPLHC (2½)
Ballygowan	1858	1950	12	03	GPLHC (2)
Shephard's Bridge	1930	1950	13	60	—
Saintfield	1858	1950	15	25	GPLHC (2)
Ballynahinch Junction	1859	1950	17	53	GPC
Crossgar	1858	1950	21	12	GPLHC (4)
King's Bridge	1929	1942	23	60	—
Downpatrick	1859	1950	26	68	GPLHC (4)
Tullymurry (1st)	1871	1896	30	40	—
Tullymurry (2nd)	1896	1950	30	73	GP
Ballykinlar	1914	1950	32	10	—
Dundrum	1869	1950	34	27	GPLHC (2½)
Newcastle	1869	1950 ('54)	38	10	GPLHC (4)

Castlewellan Branch

Station	Opened	Closed	Miles	Chains	Facilities
Castlewellan	1906	1950 ('54)	41	74	GPLHC

Donaghadee Branch

Station	Opened	Closed	Miles	Chains	Facilities
Newtownards (1st)	1850	1861	12	70	—
Newtownards (2nd)	1861	1950	13	33	GPLHC (4)
Conlig	1861	1873	15	50	—
Groomsport & Bangor *later* Groomsport Road *later* Ballygrainey	1861	1950	17	50	GP
Millisle Road	1928	1950	21	55	—
Donaghadee	1861	1950	22	20	GPLHC (2)

Ardglass Branch

Station	Opened	Closed	Miles	Chains	Facilities
Race Course Platform	1892	1950	28	05	—
Ballynoe	1892	1950	30	02	GPLHC
Bright	1925	1950	32	00	—
Killough	1892	1950	33	65	GP
Coneyisland	1934	1950	34	20	—
Ardglass	1892	1950	35	19	GPLHC (2½)

Downpatrick Loop Line

Station	Opened	Closed	Miles	Chains	Facilities
Downpatrick Loop Platform	1893	1950	26	30	—

Ballynahinch Branch

Station	Opened	Closed	Miles	Chains	Facilities
Creevyargon	1930	1950	19	20	—
Ballynahinch	1858	1950	21	20	GPLHC (4)

Note: The classification and crane power on the previous pages is abstracted from the *Official Handbook of Railway Stations*, published in 1912 by the Railway Clearing House. Abbreviations used are: G – Goods, P – Passenger and Parcels, L – Livestock, H – Horse Boxes and Prize Cattle Vans, C – Carriages by passenger train.

BANGOR—BELFAST CENTRAL—LISBURN—LURGAN—PORTADOWN

UP TRAINS—MONDAYS TO FRIDAYS

Miles from Bangor	Station codes			1	2	3	4	5	6	7	8	9	10	11	12	13	14	15	16	17	18	19	20
				LY Ftd.	06 55 BR	06 50 BR		07 25 LB		08 00 DN	CN	ED			08 25 LY	DN			LY				
				MX							L				L				L				
...	BR	**BANGOR**	dep.						06 45				07 00	07 15				07 35		07 55	08 15	08 22	08 30
1	BW	Bangor West	„						06 48				07 03	07 18				07 38		07 58	08 18		08 33
1¾	CA	Carnalea	„						06 51				07 06	07 21				07 41		08 01		08 26	08 36
2½	CB	Crawfordsburn	„						R					07 23				R		08 03			R
3¼	HB	Helen's Bay	„						06 54				07 09	07 25				07 44		08 05		08 29	08 39
4¾	SL	Seahill	„						06 57				07 12	07 28				07 47		08 08		08 32	08 42
6¾	MO	Marino	„											07 32				07 51		08 12		08 36	08 46
7¾	HW	Holywood	„						07 02				07 17	07 35				07 54		08 15		08 39	08 49
10½	SY	Sydenham	„						07 06				07 21	07 39				07 58		08 19		08 43	08 53
11	VP	Victoria Park	„						07 08				07 23	07 41				08 00		08 21			R
11¾	SD	Central Service Depot	„		06 30	06 35	06 45	07 00		07 18					07 50								
11¾	BE	Bridge End	„						07 11				07 26	07 44				08 03		08 24			08 56
12½	CL	**BELFAST CENTRAL**	arr.		06 35	06 40	06 50	07 05	07 14	07 23			07 29	07 47	07 55			08 06		08 27	08 35	08 48	08 59
...	...	„ „	dep.				07 00					07 25	07 30			08 00	08 03	08 07	08 25	08 30	08 37	08 50	09 00
13½	BT	**BOTANIC**	„				07 03						07 33				08 06	08 10	08 28	08 33	08 40	08 53	09 03
15	AD	Adelaide	„										07 37					08 14		R	08 44		09 07
15¾	BL	Balmoral	„										07 39				08 11	08 16		R	08 46		09 09
16½	FY	Finaghy	„				R						07 42					08 19		08 40	08 49		09 12
17½	DM	Dunmurry	„										07 45				08 15	08 22		08 43	08 52		09 15
18½	DH	Derriaghy	„				R						07 48					08 25		08 46			09 18
19½	LG	Lambeg	„										07 50					08 27					09 20
20	HD	Hilden	„										07 52					08 29					09 22
21	LB	**LISBURN**	arr.				07 15					07 40	07 55				08 21	08 32		08 51	08 58	09 05	09 25
...	...	„	dep.	01 25			07 16				07 25					08 11	08 22		08 38			09 06	
22	KM	Knockmore	„				07 19				07 28												
22¾	KJ	Knockmore Jct.	pass	01 30			07 21				07 30					08 13	08 25		08 40			09 09	
28	MR	Moira	dep.				07 28										08 32						
33½	LU	**LURGAN**	arr.				07 36										08 40					09 22	
...	...	„	**dep.**				07 38									08 23	08 42					09 24	
34¾	GR	Goodyear	„				07 41																
38¾	PD	**PORTADOWN**	arr.				07 48									08 29	08 50					09 32	

Extract from the NIR working timetable, summer 1977.

ACKNOWLEDGEMENTS

In my earlier book on this railway, published in 1958, I acknowledged my indebtedness to a number of persons who had helped me. Their names are all still relevant, though some of them are alas no longer with us. In addition, particular assistance has come from R. L. Beggs, D. G. Coakham and Dr. W. A. McCutcheon. The photographs taken by the late H. Fayle were made available by courtesy of the Irish Railway Record Society, and those of W. Robb by courtesy of the Belfast and County Down Railway Museum Trust.